Parenting Children with Oppositional Defiant Disorder

Navigating the ODD Journey from Challenge
Mode to Champion Mode — Fostering Self-
Regulation in Your Child

Isabella Finn

Your 2 Complimentary E-books!

Scan the QR code with the camera on your phone below to get full access or go to https://www.isabellafinn.com

Feel free to email me at isabella@isabellafinn.com

Table of Contents

Introduction

L et's be real — parenting is hard, even at the best of times. If your child has oppositional defiant disorder (ODD), it can present some unexpected and (at times) seemingly insurmountable challenges. The most important thing, of course, is that your child has a full belly, is bathed regularly, and gets enough sleep at night. However, parents of kids with ODD understand that even if they're doing a great job taking care of their child, there's no telling when that child might flip their desk at school or scream in their baby brother's ear when he's trying to sleep.

A friend of mine, Dave*, has been struggling with his seven-year-old daughter lately. Little Emma is a bright, energetic, and often challenging child who has been diagnosed with ODD. It's been a rollercoaster of emotions and experiences for Dave, and I've been there to witness the ups and downs that have come with parenting Emma.

One day, Dave told me about the previous evening in his household, which he then said was a typical one. Emma had refused to do her homework, which led to a battle of wills between them. Dave tried to stay patient and calm. He reminded her about the importance of completing her assignments, but Emma's stubbornness knows no bounds. She threw her pencil across the room and said, "I'm not doing it, and you can't make me!"

Despite his frustration, Dave knew that reacting with anger wouldn't help. Instead, he decided to use a strategy that he had learned about in therapy. He told Emma, "Okay, you don't have to do your homework right now, but we can't do anything fun until it's finished." After some

1

back and forth, Emma reluctantly agreed, and they ended up spending a tense evening with homework looming over them. Eventually, she decided to tackle her assignment, and Dave praised her for making the right choice.

This is just a glimpse of what parents of kids with ODD go through every day. It takes an incredible amount of patience to parent a child who has ODD, and even for a parent who's learned about strategies and coping techniques in therapy (like Dave), it's not easy.

*Name changed to protect privacy

Experienced parents are pretty good at rolling with the punches, but kids with ODD, in most cases, require a little extra help. Most parenting classes won't delve too deeply into this topic, which is why I've written this book to help those who are struggling with this. When your child with ODD acts out, you'll need to have the right information and tools on hand to effectively handle the situation. This is not going to be an all-encompassing guide for "curing" your child's symptoms; it's simply a tool belt for navigating the challenges that come with parenting a kid with ODD.

If you've been feeling lately like you're not a good enough parent, or like other parents are doing a better job than you are, then this book is for you. If you feel constantly overwhelmed by your child's outbursts or struggle to calm them down when they're acting out, don't worry — I've got you covered. It's important to remember, through it all, that although parenting can occasionally be grueling, the positives significantly outweigh the negatives. Raising a tiny human to adulthood is incredibly rewarding. One of these days, your kid is going to say something that blows you away, and that will make everything you've been through worth it.

The baby stage is cute (and exhausting in its own way), but it doesn't last forever. Before you know it, your child will be walking around and speaking in full sentences. They will develop their own personality and probably be disobedient now and then, which is perfectly normal. However, if your child is constantly throwing tantrums over small things and ignoring your instructions on a daily basis, they may be suffering from oppositional defiant disorder. ODD is surprisingly common, but it can be difficult to spot. It may be hard for some parents to differentiate from other mental illnesses that their child may be dealing with. It can also be difficult for some parents to acknowledge that their child has the disorder.

Most children aren't going to behave like little angels 100% of the time, but as soon as you notice that your kid is having recurrent fits of anger, you're going to want to act. Kids with ODD will frequently be disobedient or even malicious towards their parents, and while this can be challenging and hurtful, you can't take it personally. Children with ODD don't consider their behavior to be problematic, and generally don't know how to take responsibility for the problems they create.

Your child's disruptive (and occasionally rude) behavior might make you feel like you're not doing a good job as a parent. An older child with ODD will know how to weaponize this insecurity and use it against you. It's important to stay strong and not take the bait. Of course, this is easier said than done. Oftentimes, parents can't help but let their own emotions get the best of them. This can lead to explosive fights — which are avoidable.

I'm not here to tell you that you're parenting your child "wrong," or that the situation is hopeless. Neither of these things is true. By writing this book, I hope to provide you with information about how to differentiate between the symptoms of ODD and regular childhood behavior. I'll also talk about the difference between kids with ODD and kids who are simply over-emotional.

We'll also review the various treatment options for children with ODD. This book is meant to help you create a more effective parenting plan for your kid with oppositional defiant disorder. Not only will you be able to effectively manage your child's defiant behavior, but your *child* will be able to access the tools *they* need to self-regulate and calm down when they're experiencing big emotions. Keep in mind that you'll probably have to meet with a child psychologist or therapist at some point during this process — and that's okay! These resources can be quite helpful, and your child might enjoy having someone to talk to who understands them.

No matter how severe your child's oppositional defiant disorder is, it's still possible for them to lead a normal, happy life. I've spent years gathering research for this book and would like to share that research with you now. I'll also share some anecdotal stories about people I know who are currently parenting children with oppositional defiant disorder.

These stories should help you feel less alone, as well as provide you with information about how real people cope with and manage the issues you and your child are dealing with. Even after you develop a parenting plan for your child, you'll no doubt have the occasional bad day here and there. As most of us know, parenting is never smooth sailing. Despite this, I'm here to provide you with the best information and tools that I've come across. Are you ready to be the parent your child needs you to be? Let's get started!

CHAPTER 1
Understanding Oppositional Defiant Disorder

"Your present circumstances don't determine where you go;
they merely determine where you start." - *Nido Qubein,*
motivational speaker

In the beginning stages of writing this book, I found myself sitting across from my friend Dave at our favorite sushi restaurant. He told me about how a simple trip to the grocery store could be an exhausting endeavor, both emotionally and physically. On one particular trip, Emma wanted to buy some sugary cereal, but Dave tried to steer her toward a healthier choice. Emma's refusal to back down led to a full-blown meltdown in the cereal aisle. Shoppers stared, and Dave felt the weight of their judgment. As Emma began to run down the aisle, screaming and knocking over merchandise, all he could do was stand there with his mouth open, feeling helpless to address his daughter's behavior.

He tried everything to calm her down, including offering her a choice between two healthier options, but Emma was relentless. Dave finally decided to walk away from the cereal aisle, leaving his grocery cart behind. He took Emma to a quieter area in the store and calmly explained why they couldn't buy the sugary cereal. After some time, she calmed down, and they returned to the cart to finish their shopping without further incident.

I asked Dave where he learned how to parent a child like Emma. He seemed happy to talk about it with me, and I listened with rapt attention as he told me how he'd learned about oppositional defiant disorder — including what it is, what it's *not*, and some of the most common misconceptions about this complicated condition. He explained that he needed to better understand what Emma was going through so he could provide her with the support she needed, which made a lot of sense to me.

In fact, this topic captivated me enough that I later began conducting my own research, as well as talking to others in Dave's position to help me understand the nuances of ODD. In this chapter, I'll share what I've learned about what ODD is, as well as its typology. I'll explain how parents can recognize early signs of ODD (keeping in mind that not every child will display all the signs). Next, I'll explore various contributing factors and causes of ODD, as well as how it differs from other behavioral disorders. Finally, we'll review myths and misconceptions surrounding ODD that can make it difficult for parents to understand how this disorder really works.

Remember to keep an open mind and heart. After all, you're about to gain a deeper understanding of what makes your child tick! I advise you not to try and "diagnose" your child based on the signs and symptoms listed in this chapter, as a clinical diagnosis should always be given by a professional. If you're concerned, however, you can always contact a child psychologist. They will be able to provide you with guidance on developing a treatment plan for your child (something we'll cover this later in the book, as well). But now, let's get into it.

ODD: What Is It?

Oppositional defiant disorder is a behavioral condition that manifests in a persistent pattern of uncooperative, defiant, and at times hostile behavior towards authority figures like parents and teachers. This disruptive behavior can significantly impact a child's day-to-day functioning, as well as their relationships and performance in school.

It's not unusual for children, especially those from two to three years old and in their early teens, to occasionally show oppositional or defiant behavior. If you're a parent of a toddler or teen, you're probably well aware of this! These acts of defiance might include arguing, disobeying, or talking back to you and other adults. However, when these behaviors are constant for more than six months and go beyond what is considered typical for a child's age, it raises the possibility of that child being diagnosed with ODD.

Many children and teenagers who have ODD also contend with at least one additional mental health condition. These can include attention-deficit hyperactivity disorder (ADHD), various anxiety disorders like obsessive-compulsive disorder (OCD), learning differences, mood disorders like depression, and impulse control disorders.

According to Cleveland Clinic, around 30% of children with ODD may progress to develop a more severe behavioral condition known as conduct disorder (Cleveland Clinic, 2023). Without a proper diagnosis and treatment, the disruptive behaviors associated with ODD can continue into adulthood, which is just one reason early intervention is so important. We'll talk more about the importance of early intervention in the next chapter, so stay tuned!

Who Does Oppositional Defiant Disorder Typically Affect?

Oppositional defiant disorder mainly affects children and teenagers, although, in some cases, symptoms can last well into adulthood. This condition usually makes itself known by the age of eight, with most cases becoming apparent during childhood and adolescence (Cleveland Clinic, 2023). The trajectory of ODD can vary significantly. Some children may outgrow it naturally, while others benefit from appropriate treatment and interventions throughout their lives.

Interestingly, ODD seems to show some gender-related differences. Children assigned male at birth (AMAB) are more likely to exhibit ODD during their early years compared to those assigned female at birth (AFAB). However, during adolescence, the prevalence of ODD appears to affect both genders equally. Several risk factors can increase the likelihood of a child developing ODD. These include a history of child abuse or neglect, having a parent or caregiver with a mood disorder or substance use disorder, exposure to violence, inconsistent discipline, and a lack of adult supervision (Cleveland Clinic, 2023).

Additionally, family instability (e.g., moving a lot or going through a divorce) can also contribute to the development of ODD. Financial difficulties and a history of ODD, ADHD, or behavioral problems in parents may further increase the risk of a child developing ODD. This is not to say that it's your fault if your child develops (or has already developed) ODD. These things can happen for many reasons, so it's important that you look forward and learn what you can do to support your child, rather than focus on blaming yourself.

ODD Typology

Research into oppositional defiant disorder has revealed some intriguing insights into its clinical diversity. Fascinatingly, it's made clear the existence of two distinct symptom clusters within the eight criteria for ODD outlined in the *Diagnostic and Statistical Manual of Mental Disorders* (DSM). These clusters have been identified as "irritable/negative affect" and "headstrong/oppositional" (Boylan, 2014). The former appears to be associated with internalizing disorders, while the latter is more predictive of disruptive disorders. This research suggests that there could be multiple subgroups of children with ODD, which implies that each subgroup might require unique approaches to treatment.

Some studies have gone further to classify children with predominantly irritable or disruptive ODD symptoms (Boylan, 2014). The irritable group showed more comorbidity (simultaneous presence of two or more medical conditions), particularly with internalizing disorders. Nevertheless, it remains uncertain whether this group should be considered a clinical subtype necessitating a different treatment strategy. Building upon these findings, a proposed clinical typology for ODD has come up, which incorporates the contextual and developmental information that clinicians typically gather in practice. This typology includes three main types:

Stimulus Dependent ODD

This type is usually comorbid with significant ADHD and ODD behaviors across different settings (e.g., home and school). Oppositionality tends to improve when ADHD is effectively treated. These individuals often exhibit low dopaminergic tone, which tends to lead to low arousal, impaired behavioral learning, and behavioral disinhibition (Boylan, 2014).

Cognitive Overload ODD

This group faces substantial challenges in learning, language, and social processing, exceeding those seen in ADHD. As a result, they frequently meet the criteria for learning disabilities and unspecified anxiety disorders. Executive functioning (cognitive processes necessary to control cognitive behavior) difficulties tend to come up too, even under low-demand conditions. Oppositionality will often arise for reasons seemingly unrelated to environmental factors (Boylan, 2014).

Fearful ODD

This type usually includes highly aroused and stress-reactive children, who generally function well but display ODD symptoms when faced with the threat of loss or shame, typically in the presence of parents or other caregivers (Boylan, 2014). These children often have trauma histories and will exhibit characteristics associated with anxious or ambivalent attachment. Their behaviors may align closely with irritability, too.

This clinical typology remains untested. Still, it could contribute to the ongoing discussion surrounding the heterogeneity of ODD as defined in the DSM-5 (Fifth Edition). Furthermore, it sheds light on the significance of considering the context, relationship dynamics, and developmental variations that contribute to the diversity in oppositional behaviors. Clinicians will, of course, continue to explore whether their ODD patients correspond to this proposed typology, and evaluate the effectiveness of their treatment strategies in addressing specific symptoms.

Recognizing the Early Signs

Identifying the early signs of oppositional defiant disorder can be quite challenging, mainly because many of the behaviors commonly seen in children and adolescents with ODD also crop up from time to time in kids who don't have the condition. As I mentioned earlier, this overlap becomes especially noticeable during the tumultuous ages of two or three (hence the "terrible twos")and also during adolescence.

It's perfectly normal for children to occasionally display defiance, argue with their parents, or test their limits with authority figures, particularly when they're tired, hungry, or upset. What sets apart children and teenagers with ODD is the frequency and impact of these behaviors. Children and teens with ODD exhibit these behaviors more frequently, which tends to cause disruptions in their learning, school adjustment, and relationships with others (Cedars Sinai, 2023).

ODD symptoms include many different behavioral, physical, cognitive, and psychosocial signs (which, as you can probably imagine, makes it relatively difficult to diagnose kids with ODD). As a parent, it's important that you're able to spot these signs and symptoms in order to begin early intervention and to find support. Let's take a closer look at the different types of ODD symptoms below:

Behavioral Symptoms

When it comes to behavioral symptoms, children and teens (or adults, for that matter) with ODD will often show a constant defiance of rules and authority figures, whether at home, in school, at work, or within society in general (Belmont Behavioral Health System, 2023). They may frequently refuse to complete tasks — particularly in school or at work — and these refusals can be accompanied by unpredictable and intense outbursts of rage.

Additionally, ODD may manifest as aggression or hostility towards others, with children in particular starting arguments with their parents or peers, regardless of the circumstances. Another common trait among those with ODD is the tendency to blame others for their own unacceptable behavior. In some cases, they may even inflict physical or emotional harm on others, showing a lack of empathy (Belmont Behavioral Health System, 2023). Seeking revenge against those they have perceived to have slighted them is another common characteristic.

Physical Symptoms

In some cases of ODD, physical symptoms can appear, which makes things all the more complicated. These physical symptoms usually stem from the intense emotional and behavioral struggles faced by the child. One notable symptom is tension headaches, which can happen as a result of the ongoing emotional turmoil and stress that accompany defiant behavior (Belmont Behavioral Health System, 2023).

Muscle tension is another commonly observed physical symptom in those affected by ODD. The chronic emotional stress that these kids and teens go through contributes to heightened muscle tension, which often results in physical discomfort and can potentially worsen tension headaches (Belmont Behavioral Health System, 2023). People with ODD may also experience gastrointestinal discomfort, often in the form of stomach aches. These symptoms create a complex and frustrating cycle for those dealing with the condition.

Cognitive Symptoms

Children with oppositional defiant disorder also struggle with significant cognitive challenges, especially when it comes to making sound decisions. They often find it difficult to navigate situations that demand careful evaluation and planning, which can have far-reaching effects on many aspects of their lives. From academic performance to social interactions, this struggle with decision-making can lead them to make impulsive choices without fully considering the consequences of their actions.

Paying attention and concentrating (e.g., in class or on homework) is another hurdle for many children living with ODD. This can hinder their ability to effectively engage in academic settings. They may have an unusual amount of trouble focusing on tasks, following instructions, and completing assignments. The repercussions can be academic underachievement and can contribute to the frustration experienced by these children. Impulsivity is also an issue in most cases, and this can show itself in a variety of ways — from disruptive outbursts in the classroom to fights with friends and family members (Belmont Behavioral Health System, 2023).

Children with ODD also tend to have a lower threshold for dealing with aggravation or frustration. Even minor setbacks or inconveniences can trigger intense emotional reactions and spur impulsive responses. This limited tolerance for frustration can make it hard for these kids and teens to adapt to changes or manage stressors that others manage without much trouble.

Psychosocial Symptoms

Agitation and restlessness are also common feelings for children with ODD. Their inner turmoil — coupled with their frequent confrontations and defiance — leaves them in a perpetual state of unease. This inner agitation will often manifest as restlessness, which can make it a challenge to find a sense of tranquility in their daily lives (Belmont Behavioral Health System, 2023). Resentment is another emotion that frequently surfaces among children with ODD. They may carry feelings of anger and bitterness, which can be directed towards authority figures, peers, or even themselves. These emotions usually stem from a sense of injustice or from the consequences of their disruptive behavior.

Irritability and fits of rage are also common with these children and represent additional facets of their emotional struggles (Belmont Behavioral Health System, 2023). These youngsters can be easily provoked, and as I mentioned earlier, their reactions may at times escalate into outbursts of anger. Such emotional intensity can strain relationships, both with family and at school. Children with ODD may adopt a pessimistic outlook on life, which can make it even more challenging for them to build and maintain positive and constructive relationships with others as they grow older (Belmont Behavioral Health System, 2023).

Causes and Contributing Factors

The exact origins of oppositional defiant disorder remain a mystery, but experts believe a few different factors — including biology, psychology, and social dynamics — have something to do with it (Kumar, 2021). The fact that so many different factors can influence and "cause" ODD further illustrates the need for a holistic understanding of the condition. Let's take a closer look at how biological, psychological, and social factors can contribute to ODD below:

Biological Factors

Studies show that ODD may be connected to genetic predispositions and neurobiological factors. It's hypothesized that certain genetic variations or irregularities may make individuals more susceptible to ODD (Kumar, 2021). Alterations in brain structure and function might also contribute to the manifestation of ODD symptoms. Continuing to investigate these biological factors will be an important part of gaining a more comprehensive understanding of what causes ODD in children.

Psychological Factors

Psychological factors can also have a significant influence. If a child never learns how to regulate their emotions and control their impulses, this could contribute to the development of ODD. Limited ability when it comes to cognitive processes like problem-solving and decision-making can also play a role. The good news is that gaining an understanding of how these psychological factors interact with ODD could help shed light on potential therapeutic approaches (Kumar, 2021).

Social Factors

Social factors may also contribute to the development of ODD. It's been widely acknowledged that a turbulent family environment (e.g., inconsistent discipline or a lack of adult supervision) can, unfortunately, foster ODD symptoms (Kumar, 2021). Children who are exposed to violence, family instability, financial hardships, or parental mental health issues may be more susceptible to developing ODD. The influences of peer interactions, school environments, and broader societal factors are also worthy of consideration.

Personality and Temperament

Personality and temperament can play a huge role in the development of ODD. Underlying personality traits often associated with ODD include impulsivity, irritability, high emotional reactivity, difficulty in regulating emotions, callous-unemotional traits (such as emotional insensitivity and reduced empathy), and a low tolerance for frustration (Kumar, 2021). Of course, not everyone who exhibits these traits will develop ODD, which further complicates matters.

How does a child develop such personality traits, you might ask? Well, as with most things, these traits can be influenced by a combination of nature and nurture (Kumar, 2021). Biological factors contribute to a child's temperament and personality, without a doubt, but environment and upbringing can also have a significant impact. A challenging or traumatic childhood can shape a child's temperament and personality in ways that increase the likelihood of developing ODD or other mental health issues.

Curiously, people with ODD often do not perceive their behavior as defiant or oppositional. Instead, they may interpret their actions as reactions to what they consider unfair circumstances or unjust demands from parents, teachers, and other authority figures. This lack of self-awareness adds yet another layer of complexity to the condition, which further illustrates the importance of early recognition and intervention.

How ODD Differs from Other Behavioral Disorders

It can be difficult to diagnose ODD because on the surface it looks like a lot of different things (e.g., ADHD). This is why the diagnostic process for ODD is so in-depth. The symptoms of mental health conditions like ADHD, autism spectrum disorder, and conduct disorder can overlap with the symptoms of ODD as well, which makes things even more complicated. There are slight differences between these disorders, though, which we'll break down below:

How ODD Differs from ADHD

As discussed, ADHD and ODD can often co-occur in children, but it's important to understand that they are distinct disorders. It's not unusual for children to occasionally show signs of distress or defiance as they grow up and learn how to establish (and respect) boundaries. But when their defiant behaviors persist and intensify, it could be indicative of an underlying behavioral disorder (Wright, 2022).

ADHD is a neurodevelopmental disorder found in both children and adults, while ODD is a neurodevelopmental disorder that frequently occurs alongside ADHD but is more commonly found in young children and teens (Wright, 2022). To distinguish between the two, we'll need to closely examine how each condition manifests in a child's behavior.

ADHD symptoms are characterized by three main components: inattention, hyperactivity, and impulsivity. Inattention involves an inability to focus (which probably goes without saying), disorganization, and difficulty staying on task. Hyperactivity tends to manifest as restlessness, constant fidgeting, and excessive talking. Impulsivity can also be a symptom of ADHD in some cases. In contrast, ODD is primarily defined by difficulties in controlling emotions and behaviors. According to the DSM-5, ODD symptoms include a consistent pattern of an irritable or angry mood, argumentativeness, defiance, and vindictiveness toward others (Wright, 2022).

Diagnosing ADHD requires a comprehensive evaluation that considers different settings and symptoms. The diagnosis hinges on the presence of specific symptoms that disrupt daily life, taking into account criteria related to age, symptom duration, and interference with the person's social life, work, or schooling. On the other hand, diagnosing ODD requires a healthcare professional's thorough assessment, where a minimum of four symptoms persist on most days for at least six months. As previously mentioned, these symptoms usually include angry outbursts, irritability, disputes with authority figures, refusal to comply with rules, intentional annoyance of others, and shifting blame to others for one's mistakes. A milder diagnosis typically implies that the behaviors are predominantly present in one setting, while a more severe diagnosis involves multiple settings (Wright, 2022).

ADHD typically becomes evident before the age of 12. In contrast, ODD is a childhood condition that is often observed in preschool years, and its symptoms tend to decline around the age of 10 as people mature or transition into other disorders (such as conduct disorder). Interestingly, around 60% of people diagnosed with ADHD experience comorbid ODD (Wright, 2022). This comorbidity increases the risk of developing additional mental health conditions like anxiety and depression. In cases where children show symptoms of both ADHD and ODD, a holistic and comprehensive approach to diagnosis and treatment is necessary.

How ODD Differs from Autism Spectrum Disorder and Asperger's

Determining whether a child's behaviors are related to ODD or other underlying conditions, such as autism, can be a complicated process, to say the least. Children with autism spectrum disorder (ASD), including Asperger's Syndrome, may display behaviors that share aspects of ODD (The Autism Site, 2023). Communication challenges, difficulties with social interactions, and sensitivity to sensory stimuli can lead to frustration and emotional outbursts in children with ASD, though the same can be said for children with ODD, which can make it difficult to distinguish between the two. For this reason, it's important to understand the motivation behind these behaviors.

A child with ODD typically acts out with the intent to defy authority and provoke negative reactions in others. Conversely, a child with ASD may respond with genuine frustration and fear rather than deliberate defiance when confronted with situations that deviate from their familiar routines or sensory sensitivities (The Autism Site, 2023). When a child shows signs of both ODD and ASD, making a clear-cut diagnosis can be a complex process. Still, the treatment strategies for both disorders often overlap. Early diagnosis and intervention, especially when it comes to autism, are essential to alleviating symptoms and establishing effective coping mechanisms.

Children with Asperger's may also experience oppositional defiant behavior. While moodiness and a tendency to argue can be part of the normal developmental process for adolescents with Asperger's, patterns of tantrums, arguing, and disruptive behavior aimed at authority figures may indicate coexisting ODD. Approximately one in ten children with Asperger's Syndrome may experience ODD symptoms at some point during their lifetime (The Autism Site, 2023).

Typically, treating ODD involves therapy and, in certain instances, medication to address related mental health conditions. Parents need not navigate these challenges alone, as healthcare professionals and child development experts can offer specialized strategies for addressing ODD behaviors. Distinguishing between ODD and the typical developmental phases of children can be difficult and demanding, but understanding the motivation behind these behaviors — whether they stem from intentional defiance or genuine frustration — can be helpful for the diagnostic process and treatment planning (The Autism Site, 2023).

How ODD Differs from Conduct Disorder

Oppositional defiant disorder and conduct disorder are distinct but similar childhood disruptive behavior disorders. ODD, as outlined by the DSM-5, involves hostile behavior that's characterized by a constant negative mood, a quarrelsome disposition, and even vengeful tendencies that last for a minimum of six months. To receive an ODD diagnosis, a child must display at least four out of eight specified symptoms as detailed in the DSM-5, and these symptoms should manifest during interactions with people other than their siblings (The Recovery Village, 2022).

As explained earlier, ODD symptoms typically surface before the age of eight and may be influenced by factors like genetic predisposition, a lack of structure in the home, and subtle brain differences. To diagnose ODD, a mental health professional performs a detailed psychological assessment, considering the child's mental, physical, and emotional well-being, the frequency of their negative behaviors, their interpersonal interactions, mental health history, and specific criteria, including age-related considerations and an assessment of severity (The Recovery Village, 2022).

Conduct disorder, on the other hand, tends to manifest as a pattern of aggression towards others and deliberate violation of rules. The typical age of onset for conduct disorder is approximately 11 years, although it can make itself known during early adolescence, too. Symptoms include aggressive behavior, initiating fights, using weapons to harm others, acts of cruelty towards people and animals, theft, dishonesty, arson, property damage, trespassing, truancy, and other disruptive acts (The Recovery Village, 2022). For a conduct disorder diagnosis, the child or adolescent must meet a minimum of three out of 15 specified criteria within a year, with one criterion being present in the previous six months.

Despite their differences, ODD and conduct disorder share many similarities — probably more so than any other two mental disorders. It's also feasible for a child to experience both conditions, with one developing after the other. Effective treatment for both conditions is available through medical professionals, so don't hesitate to reach out to experts in your area. These disorders likely stem from a blend of genetic, environmental, and psychological factors, which again goes to show the importance of early intervention and comprehensive support.

Debunking Myths and Misconceptions

Unfortunately, children dealing with ODD often face societal stigma because of their challenging behavioral issues. This stigma can lead parents or teachers to view them as hopelessly disruptive, causing them to abandon efforts to improve the child's conduct. There can also be fear associated with the child's aggression, tantrums, or provocative actions. This, in turn, can quickly spiral into social isolation and cause additional issues like depression, thoughts of suicide, and even substance abuse (Edge Foundation, 2023).

One widespread misconception about ODD is that it exclusively affects children. While it's indeed more commonly diagnosed in children, teenagers and adults can also suffer from it. Frequently, ODD symptoms show up during childhood and may continue into adulthood if left untreated. Another misconception that it's important to dispel is that ODD solely results from trauma. While trauma can be a contributing factor, researchers now understand that ODD can be triggered by a combination of risk factors (Edge Foundation, 2023).

Another common misconception is that ODD is the result of bad parenting. Neglectful or abusive parenting *can* exacerbate ODD symptoms, but children with loving and attentive parents can also develop the disorder. How parents respond upon receiving the diagnosis significantly impacts whether and for how long ODD persists. A lot of people unfortunately believe that punishment is the most effective method to correct behavior associated with ODD, but this is definitely not the way to address it. Research has shown that punitive measures often fail to produce positive results and can even exacerbate disruptive behavior when applied inconsistently and severely (Edge Foundation,

2023). Experts recommend parent-management training as a more effective strategy to respond positively and provide discipline for inappropriate behavior.

Let's also debunk the misconception that ODD is untreatable. The truth is it can be effectively treated, with over 65% of children experiencing an improvement in symptoms within three years or less (Edge Foundation, 2023). Parents and teachers should focus on addressing the underlying conditions rather than relying solely on punishing these children for their behavior. As challenging as it may be, it's important to demonstrate patience and compassion, and show these children that they are loved and accepted, regardless of their behavior. While there is no guaranteed method to prevent ODD, research shows that positive parenting and early intervention can significantly improve behavior and prevent the condition from worsening.

Segue

Now that we've gone over what ODD is, its symptoms, and the factors that can cause it, you're ready to move on to the next chapter, which explores diagnosis and treatment. We'll discuss how to find the right healthcare professionals (it's more difficult than you might think), the importance of early intervention, how the evaluation and diagnostic process works, the different treatment options and therapies, and how to manage insurance and financial resources while working with a therapist. Let's get started!

CHAPTER 2
The Road to Diagnosis and Treatment

"Mental health is not a destination, but a process. It's about how you drive, not where you're going." - Noam Shpancer, PhD & Professor of Psychology

Many parents of kids with ODD struggle to find the proper help for their child(ren). This can be because some ODD resources aren't easy to access. It's also difficult to know where to start with treatment if the resources aren't immediately available to you, or if you don't know a lot about ODD in the first place. I'd like to share a story with you about a good friend of mine who went through several mental health professionals before finding the right one for her son.

Lisa* loved being a mom, but the experience of parenting her son Daniel, who'd been diagnosed with ODD, proved quite challenging for her, and she was determined to find the right support. I first became acquainted with them both at a neighborhood barbecue, shortly after they'd moved into my neighborhood. Daniel was an adorable eight-year-old with an infectious but mischievous grin. As we became better acquainted, I could see that Lisa and Daniel were facing some unique challenges. She told me that Daniel's ODD often caused outbursts, defiance, and stubbornness that could quickly escalate into volatile temper tantrums. Mundane tasks, like getting ready for school or completing homework would frequently spiral into lengthy battles, leaving Lisa feeling overwhelmed and emotionally drained.

Lisa tried everything in her power to help her son. She sought advice from teachers, devoured books on parenting, and experimented with therapy. But she said it was like trying to fit a square peg into a round hole. The therapist lacked expertise with ODD, and their sessions were unproductive. One day, during one of our coffee chats, Lisa couldn't hold back her tears.

"I just don't know what to do, anymore," she said, holding her head in her hands. It was clear she had reached her breaking point. She was struggling with feelings of guilt and questioning her parenting abilities. "What if I'm doing more harm than good?" she wondered aloud.

But she refused to give up on her son. At my suggestion, she dove into online research, searching for specialized therapists experienced in working with children struggling with ODD. After weeks of effort, she found Dr. Emily Turner, a child psychologist renowned for her work with children facing challenging behavioral issues. As soon as Lisa and Daniel met Dr. Turner, she felt a sliver of hope. Dr. Turner's approach was a blend of compassion and structure, and she always kept Daniel's specific needs in mind. She also introduced Lisa to techniques that prioritized de-escalation and communication over confrontation. Daniel responded positively to this approach, and before long, Lisa began to see significant improvements, and I saw Lisa relax a bit and even smile during our coffee dates.

Obviously, the path to Daniel's treatment and recovery was far from easy. There were plenty of tears and moments of self-doubt, but Lisa's resolve, as well as her boundless love for her son, ultimately led her to the right therapist — someone who understood the challenges that Daniel was going through. Watching Daniel's progress and observing Lisa's strength and dedication taught me about the power of resilience and the profound connection that exists between a parent and their child. Lisa's story is a testament to the impact that the right mental health professional can have on a parent (and family), especially one who's dealing with a complicated issue like ODD.

Because finding the right help for a child with ODD can be an uphill battle, we'll talk much more about this process in this chapter. As you'll come to learn, diagnosing ODD in children is challenging enough without having to worry about finding the right mental health professional for the job. Don't worry, though — if you set your mind to it, you should be able to find exactly what you're looking for in a therapist. Let's take a closer look at the diagnostic process, so you have a better understanding of how it works.

The ODD Diagnostic Process

Diagnosing oppositional defiant disorder tends to be a complicated process. It usually involves a thorough evaluation by a mental health provider. As we've learned, ODD often coexists with other behavioral or mental health issues, which can make it harder still (even for seasoned mental health professionals) to distinguish symptoms specifically linked to ODD from those associated with other conditions.

The assessment of a child suspected of having ODD includes several key components. Initially, the mental health provider conducts a meticulous examination of the child's overall health, to rule out any physical conditions that might be contributing to their behaviors. They will then assess the frequency and severity of the child's oppositional behaviors, which allows them to gauge the extent of the issue and its impact on the child's daily life (Mayo Clinic, 2023). The professional will also explore the child's emotional responses and behaviors regarding different settings and relationships, which provides them with a more comprehensive view of their behavioral patterns.

Family dynamics and interactions are also quite important in the diagnostic process. Understanding how the child's behaviors affect the lives of their family members (and vice versa) can help the expert get a sense of the broader impact of their condition (Mayo Clinic, 2023).

Evaluating the strategies that have previously been employed to try and manage the child's problematic behaviors is another important step in this process (to help them understand what does and doesn't work).

An assessment also considers the possibility of coexisting mental health issues, learning disabilities, or communication problems that might be complicating the full clinical picture. This multifaceted diagnostic process is meant to give the health provider a detailed understanding of the child's condition, allowing them to make an accurate diagnosis and develop the right treatment plan.

Finding the Right Healthcare Professionals

When you find yourself in the unenviable position of looking for the right mental health provider for your child, particularly when they have ODD, it can be daunting. Choosing the right healthcare professional can be overwhelming, especially if you're new to the complicated world of mental health services. So there are a few things to keep in mind.

Chances are, you'll have to meet with a lot of different mental health providers before you find the one who will best meet your child's needs. It may benefit you to learn about the difference between mental health providers, too. Psychiatrists, for example, are equipped to diagnose and treat mental health conditions, prescribe medication, and provide talk therapy (Mayo Clinic, 2023). Psychologists, on the other hand, can identify and address different mental health conditions, and can provide cognitive behavioral therapy (CBT), but they're not able to prescribe medications.

During your search, you may also come across psychiatric mental health nurses, registered nurses with training in mental health, and advanced-practice nurses who are authorized to prescribe medication according to state laws. Physician assistants can specialize in psychiatry, identify and treat mental health conditions, offer counseling, and prescribe medication when necessary. Licensed clinical social workers can provide assessment, counseling, and other services, but are not licensed to prescribe medications. Licensed professional counselors, armed with at least a master's degree, can offer counseling for mental health conditions but also do not prescribe medication (Mayo Clinic, 2023).

Family therapists are experts in family and individual therapy, so meeting with a family therapist could be a great opportunity to improve your relationship with your child. Remember to explore your health insurance coverage options, so you know which services are covered. You'll likely need to jump through some hoops to confirm whether your insurance policy covers specific mental health providers and what types of services are included. This process can be time-consuming and frustrating, but it's worth it to make sure your child has the help they need.

To find the right mental health provider, consider reaching out to your health insurance company for a list of covered professionals or ask for referrals from your primary care provider, friends, family, or people in your community. You might also want to explore options like employee assistance programs (EAPs) through your employer or mental health services at your school's student health center (if you're a student) (Mayo Clinic, 2023). National and local mental health organizations and online directories, as well as professional associations, may be able to provide some valuable recommendations, too.

When selecting a mental health provider, carefully consider their qualifications — their education, training, licensing, and how long they've been practicing. Investigate their areas of specialization and the services they offer. Do they specialize in working with children who have ODD? This isn't that common, but if you're able to find a specialist near you, you may have found your answer. This process takes time, so don't hesitate to ask questions and trust your instincts when making this potentially life-changing decision. Building a strong and trusting relationship with the right mental healthcare professional will be the key to finding effective treatment for your child.

The Importance of Early Intervention

Early intervention is important when it comes to the healthy development of children and young people, especially those at risk of facing significant challenges like ODD. The main goal of early intervention is to identify issues and provide effective support to either prevent problems from cropping up or to address them at an early stage. Basically, it's a preventative measure that can ensure a better future for your child. Early intervention not only tackles existing issues but can also set your child up with personal strengths and skills that will prepare them for adulthood.

From home visiting programs that support vulnerable parents to school-based initiatives that are designed to improve children's social and emotional skills, early intervention can encompass many different things. You might also look for mentoring programs for young people who may be susceptible to involvement in criminal activities if you're worried about your teen going down that road. While some argue that the greatest impact of early intervention is in the first few years of life, compelling evidence shows that the right interventions can improve a child's life prospects at any point during their childhood and adolescence (Early Intervention Foundation, 2023).

Early intervention can reduce risk factors while also building more protective tools for a child's life (Early Intervention Foundation, 2023). Recognizing the risk factors that can impede a child's development and increase the likelihood of them having difficulties in the future (e.g., mental and physical health issues, substance misuse, or involvement in crime) is invaluable. These risk factors are always operating at different levels within a child's environment (i.e., individual, family, community, and societal factors), and can interact in intricate ways.

Protective factors are the characteristics or conditions present in families, communities, and society that can mitigate these risks and promote the health of children and their families (Early Intervention Foundation, 2023). In many cases, risk and protective factors are intertwined. For example, a single factor could pose a risk to a child's development while simultaneously serving as a protective element against things like behavioral problems or academic difficulties. Admittedly, this can complicate the process.

Assessment and Evaluation Techniques

I touched on this briefly already, but as you're figuring out what sort of treatment your child needs for their ODD symptoms, it's important to understand how the different assessment and evaluation techniques work. Diagnosing oppositional defiant disorder is not as simple as a single test; it's a rather complicated process. This assessment includes evaluating a child's symptoms and behaviors, drawing on the professional's clinical expertise to make a diagnosis. When parents become concerned about their child's behavior, they will often initiate the evaluation process with their child's primary care physician. Let's break down the evaluation process below:

Evaluation of Medical History and Physical Assessment

The evaluation usually begins with a thorough examination of the child's medical history and a physical assessment to rule out any physical issues that could be contributing to their problematic behavior. If no physical causes are identified, the primary care clinician may refer the child to a psychiatrist or other mental health professional with expertise in diagnosing and treating mental disorders in children and adolescents. It's typically a child and adolescent psychiatrist (or another qualified mental health professional) who makes the diagnosis of ODD (AACAP, 2009).

Gathering Information from Different Sources

During the assessment, the mental health provider gathers information from parents, teachers, daycare providers, and of course, the child. Collecting information from different perspectives helps them to understand the frequency and context of the problematic behaviors and their impact on different areas of the child's life. This comprehensive information-gathering process helps the mental health provider determine the severity of the child's behavior, the nature of their conflicts (whether with peers or authority figures), and whether the behavior is linked to stressful situations at home (AACAP, 2009). It also helps establish whether the child responds negatively to all authority figures or just their parents or guardians.

The Use of Assessment Tools

Answering these questions is instrumental in helping the assessor distinguish between ODD and a response to a short-term stressful situation. Assessment tools (e.g., rating scales and questionnaires) can be useful for measuring the severity of certain behaviors. These tools can help the provider make a diagnosis, as well as monitor the child's progress during treatment. The mental health provider will also look for signs of co-occurring conditions that often accompany ODD, like ADHD, anxiety, and mood disorders. They will also examine whether your child has been involved in bullying, either as a victim or perpetrator, since this can indicate a risk for aggression and violence (AACAP, 2009).

Establishing a Relationship

Diagnosing ODD is not always straightforward, but open communication between the mental health provider, parents, and the child is crucial to arriving at an accurate diagnosis. Some children may perceive their behaviors as justified and will often lack the motivation to change. Parents may also become defensive when questioned about their parenting style — that's only natural. But building a good rapport with the mental health provider will be the key to determining whether your child's behavior stems from a temporary situation, ODD, or another behavioral condition like conduct disorder (AACAP, 2009).

Medication Options for ODD

Parents of kids with severe ODD may consider medication as a potential treatment option. Medication can work wonders for mental health issues, but it doesn't come without potential side effects and downsides. Unfortunately, this is especially true for young people who are struggling with a condition as complicated as oppositional defiance disorder. The fact that there's still a lack of research about ODD (and how medication affects it) makes this option even more complex. Still, medication can help in some cases. It may be worth some experimentation, as you switch doses or even medications a few times, because if it helps, it's worth it.

While medications aren't typically the first choice when it comes to ODD treatment, they can be useful for people with severe and treatment-resistant symptoms (Tee-Melegrito, 2023). The decision to use medication should always be a collaborative one, involving close consultation with a healthcare professional and taking into consideration the specific needs and circumstances of the person with ODD. Naturally, it's always a good idea to weigh the potential benefits of medication against the potential risks and side effects while developing a comprehensive treatment plan.

Instead of medication to treat oppositional defiant disorder, the initial approach usually revolves around psychosocial interventions like training and therapy. These methods are mainly geared toward addressing the underlying behavioral and emotional issues that characterize ODD (Tee-Melegrito, 2023). Of course, there are instances where the consideration of medication comes into play, particularly when dealing with ODD symptoms that remain unresponsive to more conservative treatments.

There isn't a specific medication that the Food and Drug Administration (FDA) has approved *exclusively* for ODD. For this reason, healthcare professionals may turn to medications that have displayed potential in managing some of the more troublesome symptoms of ODD. One category of drugs frequently prescribed for people with ODD is antipsychotics, such as risperidone (Tee-Melegrito, 2023). These antipsychotic medications come into play when behaviors such as severe aggression and disruptive conduct become excessively problematic and prove difficult to manage through other means.

Some medication treatment plans for ODD include lithium (or other mood stabilizers), especially when the individual's response to the initial intervention is only partial. This combination can be particularly effective in addressing the mood swings and emotional instability that occur with ODD. Furthermore, since ODD often co-occurs with other conditions like ADHD and depression, healthcare professionals sometimes prescribe stimulants or atypical stimulants for managing coexisting ADHD, alongside antidepressants to address coexisting depression (Tee-Melegrito, 2023). These additional medications are intended to tackle the comorbid conditions that can make managing ODD even more difficult.

Behavioral Therapy: A Cornerstone in Treatment

Oppositional defiance disorder, when left untreated or misdiagnosed during childhood, can potentially lead to long-term problems like anxiety, mood fluctuations, and behavioral issues as kids and teens transition into adulthood (Lovering, 2021). Fortunately, effective treatments are available to manage ODD, prevent its progression, and alleviate its symptoms. Of course, the first step involves obtaining an accurate diagnosis from a healthcare professional.

In diagnosing ODD, medical professionals rely on their clinical expertise to evaluate symptoms and behaviors. As mentioned earlier, they typically use questionnaires to collect information from different sources (usually parents and teachers). They categorize behaviors into three distinct groups: anger and irritability, defiance and argumentativeness, and vindictiveness (Lovering, 2021). For a formal diagnosis, whether for a child or an adult, the patient should exhibit at least four symptoms from these categories.

It's also worth mentioning again that these symptoms should persist for at least six months and have a disruptive impact on the person's social life, education, or job (if the affected person is an adult or older teen with a job). The severity of ODD is further assessed by considering the number of settings in which these symptoms manifest. They tend to be categorized as mild, moderate, or severe based on the settings involved (Lovering, 2021).

Behavioral therapy is often the best approach when it comes to managing oppositional behavior associated with ODD. When a child or teen receives an ODD diagnosis, involving parents in therapy can be beneficial, as they can learn supportive strategies for managing their kid's behavior (as well as helping their child manage their behavior on their own). Below we'll take a closer look at a few different types of behavioral therapy:

Cognitive Behavioral Therapy (CBT)

CBT, which has been proven to be effective for treating many different mental health conditions, helps people replace their challenging thoughts and behaviors with more positive and constructive alternatives. In the context of ODD treatment, CBT can help kids and teens replace symptoms like defiance and irritability with calming thoughts and positive coping strategies. This may include identifying triggers for outbursts, learning emotional regulation techniques, and monitoring their changes in emotion (Lovering, 2021).

Parent Management Training (PMT)

PMT focuses on changing parental response patterns that inadvertently reinforce unwanted behaviors in children with ODD. Parents learn to ignore attention-seeking behaviors and instead reward appropriate conduct. (Consider the example I gave of Dave praising his daughter for making the choice to do her homework assignment at the beginning of this book.) Basically, if a tantrum once led to a child getting their way, PMT training can teach parents not to give in when their child inevitably throws another tantrum.

Parent-Child Interaction Therapy (PCIT)

PCIT is specifically designed for children with ODD and offers real-time parenting coaching. Therapists will observe parent-child interactions from behind one-way glass and provide guidance through a wireless in-ear speaker. This approach allows therapists to monitor interactions as they occur and offer suggestions to parents on managing problematic behavior without their presence distracting the child. Studies have demonstrated its effectiveness in reducing behavioral problems in children with ODD (Lovering, 2021).

Collaborative Problem Solving (CPS)

CPS recognizes that children with ODD want to get along with their parents and peers but may lack the necessary skills. CPS teaches them how to communicate and compromise rather than trying to impose their will. A study involving children with ODD showed that CPS produced results either equal to or superior to parent training (Lovering, 2021). This just goes to show how well a combination of different types of behavioral therapy can work!

Peer Group Therapy

The main goal of peer group therapy (or social skills therapy) is to teach kids with ODD more effective ways to interact with their peers. This is meant to help them develop positive interactions instead of combative ones. This type of therapy tends to be most successful when conducted in a natural setting (e.g., at school).

Alternative Therapies and Complementary Approaches

In most cases, treating ODD (and similar defiant disorders) requires a holistic approach that combines the use of medication, individual therapy, group therapy, parent training, and family therapy. Residential treatment settings are often the best option for serious cases. Most parents will only consider residential treatment in a facility as a last resort, but these types of facilities can successfully treat additional problems like substance abuse, poor social skills, anxiety disorders, and other mental health issues that could be making your child's ODD symptoms worse (New Haven Residential Treatment Center, 2022).

Medication treatments will usually include stimulants to address ADHD-like symptoms and reduce impulsivity, as well as SSRIs (Selective serotonin reuptake inhibitors, the most commonly prescribed antidepressants) to treat the underlying depression that often comes with ODD. These medications not only help to reduce defiant and harmful behaviors but can also ease any internal distress your child may be dealing with. This will likely make your child more open to participating in other therapies, like cognitive behavioral therapy, social-skills training, individual therapy, and family therapy.

No matter how severe the condition is, involving family members in the treatment is incredibly important. Family systems therapy, parent training, and parent-child interaction therapy can all be very helpful, especially for teens with ODD. When parents actively participate in their child's treatment, undergo their own therapy, and commit to their family's well-being, they can greatly improve the chances of healing and growth for their defiant child or teen.

Navigating Insurance and Financial Resources

Health insurance usually covers medical costs like doctor visits, emergency room care, hospitalization, tests, and medications. The high cost of medical care is typically more than the average person can pay without insurance, but you might consider forming a group plan to make the financial aspect of care more manageable. This can spread the burden of high healthcare expenses and make getting medical care more affordable for members of the group (Immune Deficiency Foundation, n.d.).

Selecting the right health insurance plan is a major decision. The best approach is to review several different plans to find the one that best fits your needs. Dealing with insurance providers can be a complex and frustrating process, particularly when you're searching for treatment for oppositional defiant disorder, since insurance companies may deny coverage for specific treatments or services related to ODD. In such cases, you have the right to appeal their decision.

The Affordable Care Act (ACA) outlines specific rules that insurance plans must follow regarding appeals. For urgent care claims, you should receive a decision within 72 hours after requesting an internal appeal. For non-urgent care or services you haven't yet received, the timeframe is 30 days. In cases of denial for services you've already received, insurers have 60 days to respond. If you have a case manager, you can consult them to determine which mandatory appeal forms to use (Immune Deficiency Foundation, n.d.).

To start the appeal process, send a written appeal to the appropriate department, to the address provided in your denial letter or coverage documents. Work closely with your prescribing provider to include relevant clinical information about your child's health history, treatment history, and any medical records that support your case. Mention any adverse reactions or side effects your child has experienced with similar treatments. If your insurer requires a drug authorization form, make sure that your prescribing physician completes it. If your appeal relates to the medical necessity of treatment, your physician's support, in the form of a letter that includes studies supporting the treatment's benefit, could help a lot (Immune Deficiency Foundation, n.d.).

You can also request a peer-to-peer review to discuss the specific reasons for the treatment's necessity if your plan still denies your coverage. An independent external review is also an option, though this will involve professionals not affiliated with your insurance plan. To improve the likelihood of success, remember that your appeal should be brief and well-documented, as insurance companies review thousands of appeals every year. Keep it concise, since the reviewer likely has limited time for each appeal.

Segue

Now that we've gone over the diagnostic process of ODD and some of the treatment options parents tend to have success with, we're ready to move on to the next section. Going forward, remember that taking a holistic approach to your child's ODD treatment is probably going to be the best option. Medication doesn't work for everyone, but it could benefit your child if they suffer from particularly severe symptoms. In the next chapter, we'll talk about parenting with purpose, focusing mainly on holistic parenting and how to prioritize your own emotional health.

CHAPTER 3
Holistic Parenting

If you can control your behavior when everything around you is out of control, you can model for your children a valuable lesson in patience and understanding...and snap an opportunity to shape up character. - Jane Clayson Johnson, best-selling author

As you know if you're reading this book, parenting a child with ODD can take a heavy emotional toll. It's okay to acknowledge this. In fact, your acknowledgment of how difficult it can be to parent a kid with ODD can help you prioritize self-care and build a solid support network for yourself. I know what you might be thinking: "I don't really have time to practice self-care or build a support network. I've got my hands full with my kid!" I understand your reasoning, but prioritizing self-care, spending time with others who are experiencing similar circumstances, and learning how to cope with stigma and judgment from people who don't understand will help you develop your parenting style, and ultimately be the parent your child needs.

A woman I know, Maya*, has a nine-year-old daughter, Amy, who was recently diagnosed with ODD. Maya had always been strong, but Amy's ODD began to take a noticeable toll on her mental health. Before she started prioritizing her self-care and setting boundaries with Amy, Maya would frequently burst into tears when we talked. She told me her work was suffering because of the stress she was under and her boss was noticing. She even dreaded going home at the end of the day — not because she didn't want to see her daughter, but because she was afraid of her.

Many parents of kids with ODD can relate to the feeling of being afraid of their own children. This tends to be particularly true for parents of teenagers with ODD. Sometimes the weight of this condition can feel like too much. There are times when you might feel powerless against your child's rage and belligerence. You might understand that it's not their fault but might also resent them for the way they're behaving.

These are things that many parents (understandably) don't like to think about or even acknowledge. The fear and burnout that parents of kids with ODD often experience can cause them to shut down and inadvertently neglect their child's needs. This is just one reason why prioritizing self-care as a parent is so important. Time management is a factor, certainly, but by the end of this chapter, you should understand how to make time for taking care of yourself as well as your child. Let's continue.

Self-Care for Parents and Caregivers

Parenting can be incredibly stressful, and when you're a mom or dad of a child with developmental and mental health challenges, that stress can reach a whole new level. Taking care of a child with special needs can feel like a full-time job, and it can quickly become overwhelming if you don't have the right support. When parents lack the help they need, they may develop caregiver burnout, which has negative consequences for everyone involved (Garey, 2023).

The effects of prolonged stress from raising children with intense needs are significant and far-reaching. Research shows that parents of children with developmental, psychiatric, or learning disorders are more likely to experience anxiety, depression, insomnia, fatigue, and strains on their relationships (Garey, 2023). It's clear that ongoing stress takes a heavy toll on caregivers.

The emotional and physical risks to caregivers of children with behavioral challenges are not to be underestimated. Let's explore some ways you can practice self-care as a parent of a child with ODD. We'll also examine the most common sources of caregiver stress and I'll provide suggestions to help you maintain your health, balance, and commitment to your child.

Acknowledge and Accept Your Limits

Preventing burnout when caring for a child with high needs often starts with countering the belief that the responsibility of caring for this child rests solely on your shoulders, and that you shouldn't have any boundaries. Let's review advice from experts who recognize the physical and emotional toll that parents - especially mothers - can experience as a result of being a caregiver.

Dr. Wendy Blumenthal, a psychologist based in Atlanta, has met plenty of mothers who have found themselves at a breaking point due to the overwhelming sense of responsibility that comes with caring for their high-needs children (Garey, 2023). These parents, who are often affectionately referred to as "supermoms," tend to sacrifice their own sleep and comfort, constantly struggle with anxiety, and seek advice from every available medical expert.

Elaine Taylor-Klaus, co-founder of Impact ADHD (an organization dedicated to providing guidance to parents of children with conditions like ADHD), discusses the tendency for these parents to believe they should handle everything independently, often at the expense of their own well-being (Garey, 2023). This self-neglect, however, comes with long-term consequences and increases the risk of parental burnout.

To fight this burnout, Taylor-Klaus urges parents to practice self-care; for example, getting enough sleep each night, staying hydrated, making regular exercise a part of their routine, and creating opportunities for relaxation by spending time away from their children (Garey, 2023).

Ask for Help When You Need It

Asking for help, which is essential when coping with a child with behavioral difficulties, is not always easy. Parents might worry that their friends and family will not know how to provide the right kind of support. But the truth is, many of your loved ones are willing to help; they likely just need you to be clear about *how* they can help.

This process is easier when you can be direct and specific about your needs. For example, you might ask, "Could you watch the kids on Tuesday afternoon so I can go to the gym?" or "Could you do the grocery shopping next week?" These specific requests will help your friends and family understand how they can help you without feeling overwhelmed or unsure about what to do.

Dr. Blumenthal points out that people are often willing to help in small but meaningful ways. For example, they might be willing to watch your other children so you can take your special-needs child to therapy (Garey, 2023). Another helpful idea is to suggest babysitting exchanges with another parent or a network of parents who also have children with special needs. This will not only provide you with a much needed break but will allow you to gain fresh perspectives and support from people who truly understand what you're going through.

Take Care of Your Emotional and Social Health

Parents of children dealing with ODD and similar challenges often find themselves caught in a relentless cycle of caregiving that leaves little room for personal time or social connections. This demanding role can be overwhelming, and Matthew Rouse, Ph.D., a clinical psychologist, acknowledges that a significant portion of his sessions involve helping parents deal with these challenges (Garey, 2023).

While self-care tends to revolve around personal well-being, emotional and social health are equally important. Experts like Dr. Rouse highlight the importance of reclaiming an adult-only social life. This

41

can be challenging, but it's vital to your well-being as a parent. Dr. Rouse encourages parents to ask themselves questions like:

- What are you doing for yourself?
- What are you as a couple doing to support each other?
- When's the last time you had a date night?
- When did you last spend time with friends?

To cope with the sense of isolation that often accompanies parenting children with conditions like ODD, Dr. Rouse provides practical advice. He suggests looking for support networks beyond the immediate family, whether through online or in-person groups. These connections can offer you a sense of understanding and camaraderie, as well as give you a chance to share your experiences and concerns with others who understand what you're talking about (Garey, 2023).

Dr. Rouse also emphasizes the value of spending time with friends who have no direct connection to your child's challenges. While support groups can be helpful, he explains that it's equally important to have relationships that revolve around you as a person, apart from your child's condition (Garey, 2023). Parents are also encouraged to plan social activities with people who genuinely care about their happiness.

To reiterate, parents who practice self-care and build relationships outside of their child's life will be able to provide better support and care for their child over the long term. Prioritizing and practicing self-care isn't selfish but is instead a way to make sure you have more to give to your child and family as a whole.

Learn from Your Emotions

Recognizing when your emotions are taking control — instead of managing them — is a powerful form of self-care for parents of children with ODD and similar issues. Our emotions can be valuable indicators of what's happening in our life. Even your most negative or painful emotions, like guilt, anger, or resentment, can be extremely helpful. You must acknowledge your feelings, learn from them, and then take the appropriate actions if you wish to be the parent your child needs.

Caregiving is complicated, and you're bound to become emotional while doing it — especially if the person you're caring for is your own child. Some feelings are easier to handle than others, but I advise you to learn from and embrace your intense emotions rather than push them aside. For example, recognizing that your emotions are particularly intense could be a sign that you need to ask for help, that your stress levels are too high, or that you need to incorporate self-care into your daily routine.

Building a Support Network

A strong support system can be a lifeline for parents who are dealing with the complex challenges of raising children with ODD. Your support network should include people who are ready to offer help and support when you need it most. Remember that seeking this type of support doesn't signify weakness. On the contrary, having a robust social support network will equip you to effectively conquer hurdles as well as improve your problem-solving skills, which is always a plus. Your support system should give you a sense of autonomy and strengthen your self-esteem.

In today's world, building solid social relationships is more important than ever. According to the American Psychological Association's 2022 Stress in America survey, more than half of the respondents felt they could have benefited from greater emotional support since the onset of the COVID-19 pandemic (Harper, 2023). The harmful impacts of loneliness on health have grown increasingly evident. Loneliness can cause issues like elevated blood pressure, compromised immunity, cardiovascular disease, and cognitive decline. Limited social support has even been linked to a heightened risk of death from cardiovascular diseases, infectious ailments, and cancer (Immune Deficiency Foundation, n.d.).

Research continues to demonstrate that support systems can have a plethora of favorable results. They can reduce stress and physical health problems, improve emotional well-being, bolster life satisfaction, elevate self-esteem, and help us build up our resilience (Harper, 2023). By establishing a dependable network of support, parents can more easily manage the complicated and emotionally taxing journey of caring for their children while also preserving their own well-being.

Coping with Stigma and Judgment

When it comes to parenting a child with ODD, parents often find themselves grappling with an additional hurdle: the burden of stigma and judgment from people who simply don't understand. Stigma, to put it simply, occurs when one person forms a negative opinion of another based on certain characteristics, like a disability or mental illness. Discrimination takes this further, translating stigma into unfair treatment, which can include bullying behaviors like exclusion, bias, or labeling. Let's explore some strategies and approaches you can use to combat the stigma and judgment you'll likely encounter (or have already encountered) while raising a child with ODD.

Do Not Believe the Stigma

This is crucial! Often, parents with children who have ODD will experience so much stigma from others that they begin to *believe* the judgmental statements people are constantly hurling at them. When your loved ones are behaving this way, it can be especially difficult not to believe them, but you must remember to stay strong. Even those who are closest to you don't truly know what's going on in your life *or* in your child's life. A support system should never blame you for your child's ODD. That's the exact opposite of what a support system is meant to do.

Don't Let Stigma Create Shame and Self-Doubt

I am certain you're doing your best as a parent. The fact that you're reading this book right now is a testament to that. Perhaps you've done everything you can to help your child cope with their ODD symptoms and nothing has really helped. Maybe your friends have judged you or called you a "bad parent" because of what your child is going through. I'd like to reiterate that you're only *human*, and that parenting isn't easy at the best of times. Those who are judging you probably have no idea what it's like to raise a kid with ODD — and my advice is to tell them this.

Don't Equate Your Child with Their Illness

This is a common mistake parents make, and in most cases, it's not malicious. However, equating your child with their illness by saying things like "My child is ODD" may make them feel dehumanized, or like all they are is their mental illness. You would never, for example, say "My child is the stomach flu" or "My child is a broken leg." Again, this isn't usually something parents say with malicious intent. Sometimes, it's just a linguistics issue, but saying that your child *has* ODD rather than "is" ODD will benefit everyone involved.

Parenting Styles: What Works Best?

There are many different parenting styles out there. This topic has always been particularly fascinating to me, and it raises the question: which parenting style works best for children with ODD? This is an excellent question, though I can't promise I'll be able to give you a definitive answer. Very likely, the answer is: it depends.

As we know, every child is different, and a kid with ODD isn't usually going to respond to specific parenting styles (at least not in the same way that a neurotypical child would). You'll probably have to develop a healthy balance among the different types of parenting styles (excluding the "neglectful" parenting style) that I'll talk about below. It may take some time, but it'll be worth it to find something that works, don't you think?

Authoritarian

Using an authoritarian parenting style for a child with ODD can be a challenge. This style involves strict rules, obeying authority and being quick to punish if your kid isn't meeting your expectations. If you choose to use an authoritarian parenting style, your child may come to think of you as their drill sergeant — especially if you go overboard. In general, this parenting style is less nurturing and understanding than others (Pardee, 2023).

Too much authoritarian-style parenting isn't usually the best approach, but in some cases, it can be beneficial for kids with ODD, though I'd recommend using it sparingly. Even though kids might behave at home with this parenting style, they may still struggle outside the home. It can lead to problems with social skills, making decisions, and thinking for themselves (Pardee, 2023). These kids might also end up with low self-esteem, have trouble "reading" others, and struggle with anger and resentment.

Studies also suggest that there's a connection between this parenting style and more substance use in kids and teens (Pardee, 2023). The strict rules and lack of freedom associated with authoritarian parenting could make your child more likely to take risks and make poor decisions. So, while being strict might ensure that your child with ODD behaves at home, it could end up negatively affecting how they form relationships, make choices, and, overall, how they feel about themselves.

Permissive

If you choose to go with a permissive parenting style, you'll likely end up facing some unique challenges. Permissive parents often behave more like their child's "friend" than their "boss." In essence, this style is the opposite of authoritarian parenting. Parents who use a permissive parenting style tend to allow their kids to do what they want without being too strict. For example, they might let their child have soda with every meal (Pardee, 2023). In other words, permissive parents are easy going and don't have many rules compared to strict parents.

This kind of parenting can have a major impact on a child, especially if the child has a complicated disorder like ODD. Since permissive parents focus mainly on what their child wants, the kid gets used to getting everything they ask for. But there are downsides to this approach. Children who have grown accustomed to a permissive parenting style might lack responsibility and will often not receive enough help in making decisions. They may act without thinking, be aggressive, or lack independence (Pardee, 2023). All of these traits are indicative of ODD in the first place, so using a permissive parenting style can be wholly ineffective in dealing with ODD.

Even though kids raised in a permissive way might feel good about themselves, they might also act as if they deserve everything and be selfish at times. Because they don't have to work hard at home, they might not put in much effort at school, or at work later in life (Pardee, 2023). This parenting style for a child with ODD could lead to many issues with behavior. If you're able to strike a balance between permissive and authoritarian, however, you might just be able to figure out a parenting style that works well — at least, most of the time.

Authoritative

Authoritative parenting should not be confused with authoritarian parenting. This style tends to be a good middle-ground approach for kids dealing with ODD. Authoritative parents set clear rules for their children, but they also let them have some say in certain decisions (within reason, of course). They think of mistakes as chances to learn and always have clear expectations for their kids (Pardee, 2023). Even though authoritative parents are caring and warm, they also stress the importance of being responsible and disciplined.

Growing up in this kind of environment has significant positive effects on kids — with or without ODD. Kids with authoritative parents are usually confident, happy, and successful. They tend to build close, caring relationships with their parents (Pardee, 2023). That's definitely a plus! They learn a sense of responsibility, have high self-esteem, and know how to handle their feelings without becoming aggressive (of course, for kids with ODD, things are a bit more complicated). In general, though, children raised by authoritative parents are assertive, can control themselves, and take responsibility for their actions.

Children raised with authoritative parents can usually be trusted to make the right decisions on their own and set high goals for themselves. In school and in social situations, they tend to do well, and they're less likely to become involved in using drugs or alcohol (Pardee, 2023). Choosing an authoritative parenting style for a child with ODD could help them grow in a positive way and give them what they need to succeed in different parts of their life.

Neglectful/Uninvolved

Using a neglectful parenting style is pretty much the last thing you want to do. When parents are neglectful, it means they likely ignore their kids, leaving them to figure things out on their own without any clear rules or expectations. This lack of guidance from parents can damage a child's well-being, whether they have ODD or not (Pardee, 2023).

Without the right guidance, structure, or involvement from their parents, kids growing up in this environment will often act out. Studies show that children with neglectful parents are more likely to use substances, rebel, get into trouble, and have lower levels of compassion and caring about others (Pardee, 2023).

They might struggle at school or with the law and have a hard time forming strong connections with others. On top of that, these kids might exhibit signs of being depressed (Pardee, 2023), which should illustrate how detrimental this parenting style can be for any child.

Effective Communication Techniques

A child dealing with significant behavioral problems might show signs of anxiety, have frequent and intense tantrums, act manipulative, or repeatedly defy authority figures (Brain Balance Achievement Centers, 2023). Teachers, peers, and parents might label these kids as disruptive, frustrating, mean, or even "bad." If your child displays behaviors linked to ODD, you may want to try the following strategies to clearly communicate with them and handle their behavior more effectively.

Use a Calm Voice

When talking to a child who has ODD, it can help to keep your voice calm — no matter what happens. These kids often want to start arguments with you. Just say what you need to say and don't get into a long discussion with them. If you avoid the back and forth, it'll take away their chance to challenge you (Brain Balance Achievement Centers, 2023). And don't forget, the house rules apply to everyone — even parents. If you end up breaking a rule, show accountability by giving yourself a consequence, like saying you're sorry or taking a break to gather your thoughts. Kids with ODD might see themselves as victims, so setting an example by apologizing and following the rules could help them understand that the same is expected from everyone in the family.

Celebrate Your Child's Successes

Kids with ODD often find it difficult to handle their emotions. This can lead to intense tantrums. So, when your child does a good job keeping their behavior in check for a longer period of time, it's a big deal and deserves some celebration (Brain Balance Achievement Centers, 2023). Maybe treat the family to a nice dinner at their favorite restaurant or reward your child with a new toy. Let them know that you see and appreciate the extra effort they're putting in. Taking the time to enjoy happy moments and connect when your child is feeling calm and doing well is extremely important. It helps build on their good behavior and creates a positive family atmosphere (which for kids with ODD is crucial).

Set Rules and Enforce Them with Consequences

Making and sticking to rules is a big part of communicating more effectively with your child who has ODD. Kids with ODD often struggle with feeling anxious and want to be in control of what's going on around them. Therefore, it's important to keep your rules simple and not overload their brain with information (Brain Balance Achievement Centers, 2023). The rules you set could just be basic stuff, like not hurting themselves or others, and using kind words without being too loud. Posting these rules (perhaps with a magnetic whiteboard that you hang up on your fridge) and deciding beforehand what will happen if your child breaks a rule will help them understand the consequences.

Once a rule has been broken and the consequences have been meted out, it's important to let go and move on. This will show your child that every new day is a chance to do better. By keeping things clear and sticking to the rules, parents can create a supportive environment for their child with ODD. It's a great way to make sure they understand the correlation between rules and consequences — and might just inspire them to think twice before making bad decisions in the future (Brain Balance Achievement Centers, 2023).

Segue

Clearly, holistic parenting can be a bit of a juggling act. It takes getting used to, and chances are you'll hit a few bumps in the road. If your child with ODD isn't used to holistic parenting methods (like a combination of authoritative parenting and permissive parenting, for example), it may take a while for them to adjust to the changes. Ultimately, though, parenting holistically will be beneficial for not just your child, but for you and your partner (if applicable), too. In the next chapter, we'll talk about nurturing emotional intelligence in kids with ODD. If you've been wondering how to teach your child about how to cope with their feelings, build skills for empathy and conflict resolution, and develop resilience, this is a chapter you might want to bookmark.

CHAPTER 4
Nurturing Emotional Intelligence

"It is not what you do for your children, but what you have taught them to do for themselves that will make them successful human beings." - *Ann Landers*, advice columnist

The other day, my friend, Riley*, was telling me about this new method she was trying with her son, Cody, who'd been diagnosed with ODD almost two years ago. Cody was a rambunctious and bright, but occasionally belligerent, 11-year-old. Riley had the sense that, beneath all the screaming matches and tantrums, there was a child in Cody who was trying to connect with her on an emotional level. Cody didn't understand his intense emotions, though. Because of his ODD, he wasn't able to express complicated emotions like anger and fear in healthy ways. This led to him lashing out at his mother every time he felt scared or upset about something. Not knowing what to do with his emotions — essentially not knowing where to "put" them — he ended up putting them onto his mom, dad, and younger sister. This caused turmoil in the family, and Riley knew that something had to be done about it.

She told me she'd been reading about the benefits of teaching kids emotional intelligence. Her face lit up as she talked about the importance of listening to your children when they're upset, expressing empathy and understanding regarding why they're upset, and allowing them to express their emotions in a safe space and in a safe way.

I've been able to see firsthand the progress that Riley and Cody have made together. Riley's patience and determination have not only helped Cody understand himself better but have also provided him relief from some of the symptoms associated with his ODD. Now that Cody is beginning to have a better grasp of why he feels upset — and is able to acknowledge the fact that his bad feelings won't last forever — he's become quite good at regulating his emotions. Again, because Cody has ODD, he has to work extra hard to be able to effectively regulate his emotions, but he knows his mom is on his side, which makes everything a bit easier.

*Name changed to protect privacy

In this chapter, we'll be delving into the power of emotional intelligence and review some strategies you can use to further enhance your child's emotional intelligence. It's going to take time, of course, so you'd do well to hone your patience and develop your own emotional intelligence skills as well. You may already be quite emotionally intelligent. Some people are gifted in that way. Your child may also be emotionally intelligent, even if they do have ODD, but their symptoms are blocking them from being able to properly *express* their emotional intelligence. This chapter is intended to provide you with some ways to help your child discover their emotional intelligence and more effectively cope with the symptoms that may be preventing them from expressing their emotions in a healthy way. Let's begin.

Emotions 101: Teaching Kids About Feelings

Understanding and managing emotions is incredibly important for kids (especially those with ODD). As children go through the ups and downs of life (as we all do), they must deal with all kinds of feelings that can sometimes be difficult to understand, let alone handle. Being able to figure out, understand, and cope with their own emotions in a positive way is incredibly beneficial. When we teach our kids how to do this, we're giving them the tools they need to cope with stress, build good relationships with others, and handle different social situations.

Kids who are emotionally intelligent are usually very well adept at regulating their emotions. It can be difficult even for adults to regulate their emotions, so this is not inconsequential. By teaching your child the skills that build emotional intelligence, you'll be giving them the strength they need to deal with stressful or upsetting situations in a healthy, non-disruptive way.

Since we haven't yet defined it, emotional regulation means figuring out how to manage and control your feelings in response to things happening both internally and externally. Having emotional intelligence makes it easier to self-adjust and determine how strong your feelings are. It's easy to see how this would be a useful skill for kids with ODD. There are plenty of strategies involved when it comes to emotional regulation. Your child will need to learn how to calm themselves down, look at things from a different perspective, and solve problems on their own. Unfortunately, for a child with ODD, this is easier said than done.

Still, though, teaching emotional intelligence and regulation to a child with ODD is possible. They may struggle at first, because as we've learned, they may not know exactly how to express their strong emotions yet. Be patient and empathetic, give them the right words to talk about how they're feeling, and praise them when they show signs of emotional intelligence and self-regulation. We'll review some emotion-regulation strategies later, but for now let's learn about the intricacies of Social Emotional Learning (SEL).

Social Emotional Learning

Understanding and embracing SEL is a big deal when it comes to parenting and educating kids with ODD. Teachers often have to deal with students becoming frustrated in class, and some kids even question why they have to learn something. We've all been there as students, wishing we had clear explanations about why a subject matters, and how it connects to our lives outside school and in the future. Kids need to learn how to deal with this frustration and construct positive ways to handle their emotions, as well as interact respectfully with others. This is where SEL enters the picture (National University, 2022).

In today's world, classrooms are where most children first meet people with different backgrounds, abilities, and beliefs. To make sure all students can do well, SEL must be utilized — by parents and teachers alike. It allows students to better understand their thoughts and feelings, which helps them become more aware of themselves (as well as more understanding of others). The goal is to create a space where every student, no matter who they are and what they're going through, can succeed (National University, 2022).

When teachers bring SEL into their lessons, they're not focusing only on grades. They're attempting to build qualities that go beyond academic success. Things like knowing yourself better, understanding others more, and being more caring in general are all parts of Social Emotional Learning (National University, 2022). The idea is to shape students into not just intelligent individuals, but also into good citizens who are able to make positive contributions to society.

SEL lays the groundwork for kids (with or without ODD) to be able to handle relationships and emotions in a more effective and efficient way. These skills go beyond the classroom, because they can be applied to all parts of life. This is why embracing SEL is so valuable — ultimately, it will help your child become a well-rounded person who's able to thrive in a variety of situations.

Emotion Regulation Strategies

Of course, regulating your emotions isn't always easy. It may come naturally to some adults, but everyone has to learn how to do it at some point. This is why adults tend to be better at it than most kids and teens — they've simply had more practice. For some people, figuring out how to regulate their emotions is a lifelong journey, and that's okay! For a child with ODD, it can be especially difficult. Thankfully, there are some strategies you can use to help your child develop their own emotion regulation skills. Let's take a look at some of these now:

Acknowledge What Your Child Is Going Through

When you're helping your child become more emotionally aware, recognizing and acknowledging their point of view is critical. Even if you can't fix what's bothering them right away, just showing them that you understand can make a big difference. If they feel like you "get them," this will create a safe space for them to express their feelings and should make it easier for them to let go of whatever is upsetting them (Markham, 223). Sometimes a child's upset feelings might seem bigger than the issue at hand (although, to them, the smallest thing might feel like the end of the world) because people (especially children) tend to build up their feelings and then let them out when they feel safe.

Empathy, in this situation, doesn't mean you have to agree with everything your child feels; it just means you understand their perspective. Even if your child has to follow certain rules, acknowledging their perspective reminds them that their feelings matter and are valid (Markham, 2023). Everyone appreciates when others are able to see things from their viewpoint, and this recognition can make it a bit easier for kids with ODD, in particular, to handle situations where things don't go their way.

Saying things like, "It's tough for you to stop playing and come to dinner, but it's time now," or "You really want to have me all to yourself, huh?" can help to build a stronger connection with your child. These empathetic responses let your child know that you understand what they're going through emotionally. When you give your child the space to talk about their feelings and connect them to specific situations, you won't just be acknowledging their perspective; you'll also be helping them learn how to cope with their emotions (Markham, 2023).

This process triggers the release of calming chemicals in the brain, which helps to strengthen the pathways that will help your child soothe themselves as they grow older. Needless to say, it's incredibly important for children to experience empathy from others, as this is what will help them learn how to be empathetic themselves (Markham, 2023). By acknowledging your child's emotions, you'll be giving them the tools they need early on to deal with emotions like anger and fear (emotions commonly and frequently experienced by kids with ODD). It's a great way to encourage self-awareness and help build the foundation for your child to hone their emotional intelligence and emotion regulation skills later in life.

Allow Your Child to Express Their Emotions

When helping a child with ODD manage their emotions, it's important to let them express how they feel, as this helps promote healthy emotional growth. Understanding that these little ones may struggle to separate their emotions from who they are is key. Instead of brushing off or belittling their emotions, embrace them. This will show them that all feelings are valid, and, in time, they may even be able to reject the idea that certain emotions are embarrassing or off limits (Markham, 2023).

Telling a child not to feel fearful or angry doesn't magically erase those emotions. In fact, it might push them to hide them from you, which obviously isn't healthy. Unlike freely expressed emotions, hidden feelings tend to stick around and find ways to come out uncontrollably. This might look like aggression toward siblings, frequent nightmares, or the development of nervous habits (Markham, 2023). To avoid this, emphasize to your child that experiencing the entire range of human emotions is a normal part of being human. Be sure to clarify that it's okay to feel a certain way, but how we act on our feelings is what matters most.

This can be a difficult concept for a child to understand. Dr. Laura Markham, a clinical psychologist, emphasizes that a constructive way to approach this is by recognizing and putting into words your child's emotions. For example, saying, "You're so mad your brother broke your toy! I get it, AND it's never okay to hit, even when you're really mad. Tell your brother in words how you feel," helps the child understand their emotions while also setting clear boundaries for acceptable behavior. Similarly, showing understanding about their worries or frustrations by saying things like, "You seem worried about the field trip today. I used to get nervous on field trips too. Want to talk about it?" opens up opportunities for communication (Markham, 2023).

By acknowledging and accepting your child's emotional experiences, you can help build their emotional intelligence as well as enhance their ability to regulate their emotions. Your acceptance of their emotions will not only help your child recognize and embrace their own emotions but will also give them the space and tools they need to manage their emotions effectively (Markham, 2023). Basically, you send the message that their emotional life is not something dangerous or shameful, and this approach reinforces the idea that your child needs to be fully accepted for who they are, even when they're going through emotional challenges.

Listen to Your Child

This one may seem obvious. Perhaps you're saying, "Well, of course! I always listen to my child!" But there's a difference between "listening" and "active listening," and your child with ODD will benefit more from the latter. Keep in mind that your child's intense emotions – like rage, for example — won't start to ease up until they feel acknowledged and heard. Whether your child is a little six-month-old or a teenager, they want you to tune in to the feelings they're trying to express. Allowing them the space to feel and express these emotions will help them move forward from whatever is causing them distress. Surprisingly, once given the chance to let it out, children will often become more affectionate and cooperative (Markham, 2023).

Now, creating a safe space for your child to release their emotions is sometimes easier said than done. Your child needs to be able to sense that you're fully present and actively listening. If you have a lot going on in your life (i.e., work, relationships, other children, etc.), this could make it more difficult for you to fully and actively listen when your child is trying to tell you about their emotions. That's why it's so important to give them frequent assurance. As a parent, your role is to allow them to express themselves while resisting the temptation to make their painful emotions vanish (Markham, 2023). When they're given the space to do so, your child will learn how to heal themselves.

Using empathetic and understanding statements like, "You seem so unhappy right now. Everybody gets upset sometimes... I'm right here. Tell me about it," or, "You are so sad and mad, you just want to scream and yell and cry. Everybody feels that way sometimes. I'm right here listening and see all of your big feelings. You can show me how mad and sad you are," is an effective way to create opportunities for your child to express themselves. This approach will allow them to simply experience their emotions and let them flow freely. They shouldn't feel like they need to stifle them or pretend to be "happy."

By helping your child feel secure enough to experience and express their emotions, you'll not only be contributing to their immediate well-being, but you'll also be playing a role in building their trust in their emotional process (Markham, 2023). This foundation of trust will help them cope with their emotions as they grow, decreasing the likelihood of tantrums or emotional repression (once they age out of tantrums, that is). As a parent, you're responsible for guiding them toward a healthier relationship with their emotions, and, in turn, nurturing the emotional intelligence that already exists within them.

Play It Out

This method might seem a little strange, but just bear with me. When you notice that your child is struggling with overwhelming emotions that they might not know how to handle, "playing" through their emotions can sometimes be a helpful approach. Dr. Markham offers the example below.

Let's say you're Dad and notice that your four-year-old consistently shows a strong preference for Mom. Rather than taking it personally, you can use play. Make it into a game by pretending to try to keep them away from Mom. You might say, "I won't let you get to Mom... Hey, you just ran right around me!... You pushed me right over!... You are too strong!... But this time you won't get past me!" This lighthearted interaction should make your child giggle, boast about their abilities, and, most importantly, release any pent-up worries that may be behind their constant demand for Mom (Markham, 2023).

Promoting play as a method of emotional expression and resolution aligns with how children naturally handle big feelings. Through play, your child will not only have a good time in the moment but will also be able to process their emotions in a symbolic way (Markham, 2023). Making it into a game helps create a safe space for your child to express and work through their emotions.

As I mentioned earlier, children with ODD may find it challenging to put their deeper emotional conflicts into words. However, through symbolic play, they can act out and resolve these conflicts without the need for any explicit conversation (Markham, 2023). Further, the laughter element in play can provide your child with stress relief. Obviously, playing with your child is also an excellent way to bond with them. Honestly, it's a win-win situation for everyone involved!

Cultivating Empathy and Compassion

As most of us probably know, empathy is the ability to understand and share others' feelings. Compassion is what we use when responding to someone who has shared emotions or hardships with us. It's a form of active listening that makes those with whom we interact feel seen and heard. Both empathy and compassion are learned skills. By honing them, children and adults alike (including those struggling with ODD symptoms) cannot only experience increased happiness but may also witness improvements in their personal relationships.

Developing empathy and compassion isn't just a nice idea; it's a practical strategy that can significantly improve one's emotional well-being. Cultivating empathy and compassion is particularly critical when parenting a child with ODD. Encouraging your child to prioritize others isn't just a moral lesson; it enhances their personal growth and emotional development (Weil, 2023). Not only does this approach reduce social isolation, it actively works against self-centered tendencies. This is great news for parents of kids with ODD.

Former Peace Corps volunteer and author, Allan Luks, originated the term "helper's high," a concept that describes the emotional rewards that stem from helping others. Scientifically, acts of kindness trigger pleasure centers in the brain. People who engage in acts of kindness are not only less prone to depression, but are also more likely to experience happiness, as evidenced by findings from the Social Capital

Community Benchmark Survey. This survey revealed that those who contribute their time or money to others are 42% more likely to report feelings of happiness (Weil, 2023).

For children who are struggling with ODD, instilling empathy and compassion is critical to fostering emotional well-being. This process involves both thought and action, from participating in volunteer efforts to simply heightening awareness of others' struggles and dedicating time and energy to alleviate their pain (Weil, 2023). Even seemingly small gestures, like sharing a toy with a friend, can come with surprising emotional benefits for children (with or without ODD). The proven connection between kindness and personal happiness is a testament to the power of cultivating empathy.

Conflict-Resolution Skills

You've probably heard the term "conflict resolution" many times, especially if you work in an office. But it may surprise you to know that kids can learn conflict-resolution skills, as well, and for children with ODD, these skills can prove extremely useful. When emotions are running high, most kids with ODD are going to have trouble self-regulating and solving problems. When another person is involved, this can further complicate matters. This is where conflict resolution comes in handy.

Teaching a child with ODD conflict-resolution skills can be tricky. They may be reluctant to listen or refuse to take the process seriously. It's important to keep trying, though, because conflict-resolution skills could serve as a tool that your child can use — both at home with their siblings and at school with their classmates. I recommend using tools like a feelings chart or a stoplight system. Red means it's time to cool off, yellow shows that things are calming, and green means they're ready to work on the problem (Garey, 2023). Help your child find ways to calm down, such as playing with a pet or simply taking some deep breaths.

Once they're ready to focus, help them figure out the real issue that's causing the conflict. It might not just be about what started the fight. Encourage them to suggest solutions and point out that the best choice is going to be the one that matches their feelings and helps them achieve their goal (whatever that may be). Even if their ideas don't work out perfectly, give them praise for trying to fix the problem. This will encourage them to keep trying to resolve the conflict (Garey, 2023). Let's take a closer look at some conflict-resolution skills that you can teach your child:

First Things First: Tackle Feelings

Navigating conflicts is never easy, especially for children with ODD who are often grappling with intense emotions. Before getting into the specific issue causing the conflict, such as a disagreement over a toy or a friend's betrayal, children must be able to attain an emotional state that allows for rational thinking (Garey, 2023). This will help prevent them from making impulsive decisions that might worsen the situation.

Visual tools, recommended by child psychologist Stephanie Lee, PsyD, and clinical social worker Carey Werley, LCSW, can be quite helpful when it comes to teaching your child(ren) conflict resolution skills (Garey, 2023). For younger kids, a visual-feelings chart featuring illustrations of different emotions can be beneficial. Magnetized charts placed on the refrigerator could serve as practical aids in helping children identify their feelings.

Another effective visual tool is the stoplight system, mentioned earlier. This is particularly useful for younger children. This system provides a clear indication of emotional intensity. A child pointing to the red zone signifies emotions too intense for immediate conflict resolution. Yellow signals a diminishing emotional intensity, and when they reach the green zone, children are prepared to engage in conflict resolution skills (Garey, 2023). Again, the main goal is to guide children away from actions that could escalate or exacerbate the situation.

Figure Out What the Source of Conflict Is

After the intense emotions have settled, the next step is getting to the root of the problem. Of course, younger children may lack the emotional awareness to identify what actually sparked the conflict in the first place. In these situations, kids might need some help in understanding the underlying reasons behind their disagreements. Take, for example, a scenario where your child and their friend are arguing over a toy – the real issue might go beyond the immediate conflict. As Carey Werley points out, it could be linked to broader concerns, like one of them making a new friend while the other feels left out (Garey, 2023).

Guiding your child with ODD to uncover the root cause of whatever problem they're having a hard time dealing with may serve not only to resolve the current conflict but could also provide them with skills to identify and discuss similar issues in the future. Older kids, usually those in grade school and middle school, are more likely to have the language skills needed to pinpoint the source of conflicts (Garey, 2023). With some guidance, they can learn to independently apply these skills when dealing with challenges in the future.

Come Up with Solutions Together

Once your child is able to grasp the issue at hand, the next step is guiding them toward potential solutions. While younger children may require more support from their parents, older kids and teenagers can still benefit from having someone with whom to discuss ideas. Dr. Lee proposes a systematic approach for both age groups. She suggests engaging in a collaborative brainstorming session to explore different solutions. From there, you can work together to choose the most appropriate one (Garey, 2023).

If your child is really struggling with problem-solving, Dr. Lee suggests playing a game of "problem-solving baseball." This helps make the problem-solving process a little more fun and accessible. Lee describes the process: "I have kids pitch me a problem, and then we go through the bases. First base is identifying the problem, second base involves exploring potential options, third base is narrowing down the best options, and home plate is evaluating whether they made the right decision. The goal is to help even very young kids understand what will get them closer to their goal" (Garey, 2023).

Now, it's often going to be difficult for kids with ODD to know what the best option is. Kids and teens with ODD tend to lack problem-solving skills in the first place, so it takes practice (as well as some trial and error). Your job is to communicate to your child that the goal is to put forth their best effort rather than immediately come up with a flawless solution (Garey, 2023). If their first idea for a solution doesn't work out, they may need to go back to the drawing board. This can be frustrating, but remind them it's just a part of the problem-solving process. In time, they will come to understand this, even if they suffer from ODD.

Positive Discipline Techniques

Raising a child with ODD requires a thoughtful and supportive approach to discipline. You're probably well aware of this already, and may be asking, "Okay, but *how* do I use this so-called thoughtful and supportive approach? What if my kid still doesn't listen?" Despite the hurdles that come with this disorder, you must recognize and acknowledge the fact that a child with ODD can also be smart, creative, and caring — just like any other child. Using positive discipline techniques *can* help to improve their behavior over time, but it's going to — you guessed it — *take time*. As long as you understand that huge improvements won't happen overnight, you should be prepared to start using positive discipline techniques with your child who has ODD.

One strategy that experts recommend is to give your child daily doses of positive attention. Since children with ODD often find themselves navigating more negative interactions with others, spending at least 15 minutes each day on positive, quality attention can make a real difference. Participating in activities together — like playing games or working on a project — will not only strengthen your bond but may also reduce their tendency to try to get your attention by acting up or picking fights with siblings (Morin, 2020).

Setting clear rules and boundaries is also extremely important. Children with ODD may question the rules much of the time, and older kids with ODD may search for loopholes or express concerns about fairness (Morin, 2020). To address this, you'll want to create straightforward household rules, write them down, and put them in a visible place. When conflicts occur, you can refer to the rules and hopefully cut down on arguments. This will also help create some consistency in your child's life, which, for kids with ODD, can be very helpful.

You may also want to come up with a behavior plan that's specifically tailored to your child's specific challenges. This means figuring out consequences for rule-breaking, and communicating these consequences in advance (Morin, 2020). At the same time, remember to make a big deal out of the fact that there will be positive consequences for good behavior. Reward systems — like giving your kid a gold star sticker (with a certain amount of gold stars earning them a treat) every time they share with their siblings or do their chores without complaining — can be extremely effective for children with ODD.

Consistency with consequences is key. If there aren't consistent negative consequences for bad behaviors, your child will have a difficult time improving (Morin, 2020). Avoid power struggles with them by giving them clear instructions and explaining the consequences of their actions *without* getting into a lengthy debate with them about it. This is important, because chances are your kid with ODD *will* try to pull you into a debate! Also remember that understanding the reasons behind your child's behavior is more important than making things unpleasant for them. This compassionate approach may take some practice (and a great deal of patience), but it'll be worth it in the long run.

Building Resilience and Coping Skills

Being able to bounce back from difficult situations or circumstances (having "resilience") is an absolute must for parents and kids who have been affected by ODD (*Resilience: Build Skills to Endure Hardship*, 2022). When dealing with the stresses that come with your child's ODD, you'll probably feel like you're emotionally, mentally, and, on occasion, physically, being put to the test. You're probably no stranger to this, and as I've said, if you *do* feel emotionally drained, you're certainly not alone.

Many think that being resilient simply means being able to overcome anything by being stoic, but in reality, resiliency is about being able to adapt to circumstances that are outside of one's control. In the face of things like stress, adversity, or trauma (all of which ODD can cause), you'll probably experience emotions like anger and grief. Being resilient (i.e., managing to function both physically and mentally despite what you and your child are going through) takes a lot of strength, but you don't have to do it alone. In fact, asking for help is an important aspect of building resilience (*Resilience: Build Skills to Endure Hardship*, 2022).

The connection between resilience and mental health runs deep, especially for parents of kids with ODD. Building resilience is important because it can be a shield against mental health conditions like depression and anxiety, and can help you cope with factors that increase the risk of such conditions (e.g., being bullied at work, or being triggered by something that reminds you of a past trauma) (*Resilience: Build Skills to Endure Hardship*, 2022). For parents already dealing with mental-health conditions, building their resilience can be a lifesaver.

To improve your resilience as a parent of a child with ODD, it's generally recommended that you build strong, positive relationships with loved ones (*Resilience: Build Skills to Endure Hardship*, 2022). After all, everyone needs a solid support system to help them cope during difficult times. Making connections through volunteering in your community or attending a support group could also be an effective way to build resilience. It's also a good idea to come up with goals — big and small — that you want to solve by the end of the day, week, month, and year. Feel free to start small, though! The last thing you want to do is accidentally overwhelm yourself.

No matter what happens, do your best to stay hopeful. In fact, that's one of the most important aspects of resilience! While the challenges of ODD can be overwhelming for both you and your child, accepting and anticipating change can make it easier for you to adapt and deal with new challenges — and with less anxiety, too (*Resilience: Build Skills to Endure Hardship*, 2022). Remember, though, to take care of yourself. You might feel like parenting your kid with ODD is taking up all of your time, in which case, you may want to reach out to your support system for help. If you can't take care of yourself, you're probably going to have a difficult time taking optimal care of your child, right? This will be hard for some parents to accept, but it's true — not taking care of yourself while taking care of your child isn't sustainable for the long term.

Segue

When parenting a child with ODD, it's not only important that you focus on improving your child's emotional intelligence, but your own emotional intelligence as well. This will give you the strength you need to be patient and compassionate, despite how your child is behaving at any given moment. Now that you've learned some emotion regulation strategies — like playing it out, allowing your child to express their feelings, active listening, and acknowledging what your child is going through — you're ready to start helping your kid with ODD face their demons and gain some independence when it comes to self-regulation.

You should also feel better equipped to teach your child how to use conflict-resolution skills. Remember, both you and your child will benefit from coming up with creative solutions together! In the next chapter, we'll discuss the art of establishing clear boundaries. And children thrive on routine, especially those with ODD, so we'll also explore ways to create a consistent routine for your child.

CHAPTER 5
Consistency in Boundaries

"Children raised with good boundaries learn that they are not only responsible for their lives, but also free to live their lives any way they choose, as long as they take responsibility for their choices. For the responsible adult, the sky is the limit." - *Henry Cloud,* psychologist and best-selling self-help author

In today's fast-paced world, where everything is at our fingertips and instant gratification has become the norm, parenting has become more complex than ever before. Our children are growing up in a society that rarely advocates for patience and often leans toward the idea that they should get what they want simply because they're here (Abraham, 2023). This shift in attitude is something that many parents find challenging, but for those bringing up kids with ODD, these issues can be especially pronounced.

I have a friend, Sophie*, whose 14-year-old was recently diagnosed with ODD. Her daughter, Chloe, is a force to be reckoned with. Not only does she constantly talk back to her mom, but she's even been in trouble with the law a few times. Money has been mysteriously disappearing from Sophie's wallet, and when she confronted Chloe about it, it devolved into an all-out screaming match. Sophie told me that things eventually got to the point where she was afraid to confront Chloe and felt like she had no choice but to let her daughter walk all over her.

Kids and teens with ODD, given their low tolerance for frustration, limited coping skills, and impulsive nature, often believe that their desires should be fulfilled instantly (Abraham, 2023). So, if Chloe asked her mother if she could go out with her friends, and Sophie responded with something like, "Yes, if you clean your room first," there would be a huge blow-out between them. The mere thought of disappointment or not getting what she wanted would cause Chloe to unleash a barrage of verbal abuse upon her mother — swearing, name-calling, yelling, intimidation, threats, and general demeaning behavior that would leave any parent feeling as if they'd just been hit by a tsunami.

Sophie told me she understood that she had to start setting boundaries with her daughter. She wanted, more than anything, to connect with Chloe, but Chloe seemed completely averse to the idea — at least at the time (her age likely had something to do with this). For the time being, the best thing Sophie could do for her own mental health was establish some boundaries with Chloe. She had to make it clear that she wasn't okay with Chloe treating her like a doormat and stealing money from her. She had the words ready in her mind, but fear took hold. She also wasn't sure how to get Chloe to face the consequences of her bad behavior. When Sophie told me about how much of a headache the whole process was, I decided to do some research for her — and this is what I'll be sharing with you here.

In this chapter, we'll dive into the (seemingly insurmountable but not impossible) task of setting boundaries and establishing routines when raising a child who has ODD — a task that Sophie, thankfully, was eventually able to tackle head-on. These strategies are not only critical for bringing structure and discipline to your household but might also help to create an environment where both you and your child are able to manage the challenges of modern expectations and ODD-related behaviors. There's a delicate balance of discipline, compassion, and understanding, and the key to parenting a child with ODD lies in discovering that balance. Let's get into it!

The Importance of Setting Clear Boundaries

Setting boundaries can be especially difficult when you have a child with ODD, since they will often be reluctant to respect these boundaries. Still, setting boundaries is both possible and necessary. Just remember to stick to your guns, no matter what happens. Keep in mind that you might have to deal with your child throwing verbal abuse your way (as Sophie did with Chloe), and this will likely take an emotional toll on you. It will be uncomfortable, especially at first, but it's important to address this issue directly.

Verbal abuse will often become a repetitive pattern within the family dynamic of someone with ODD. When faced with discomfort or being denied their wishes, a child with ODD might respond in a verbally aggressive way. Try not to take this personally (easier said than done, I know), because your child is likely verbally abusing you out of frustration, anger, or an attempt to manipulate you due to their ODD. How you react in this situation is crucial. Unfortunately, tolerating or even reinforcing verbal abuse can become habitual, and this can lead to lasting negative consequences (Abraham, 2023).

To disrupt this pattern and put an end to this type of behavior, you'll need to identify and communicate your boundaries clearly with your child. Calmly express to them what behavior is acceptable and what isn't (for example, you might explain that swearing or yelling won't be tolerated). Clearly outlining and discussing these boundaries with your child will help to improve your parent-child relationship. You'll also need to be explicit about the consequences they will face if they cross these boundaries. Real-world repercussions, like withholding privileges, can teach children with ODD about the outcomes of their actions. They need to understand that verbal abuse *won't* result in them receiving special treatment or rewards. This, after all, mirrors how things work in the real world, and will help them grow into more successful adults (Abraham, 2023).

Consistency is key when enforcing these boundaries. If you aren't consistent with disciplining your child, they may begin to believe that their actions are acceptable. This will only reinforce their belief that verbal abuse is a way to get what they want. Setting and sticking to your boundaries is a way to teach your kid(s) about respect, responsibility, and facing the consequences of their actions. As a parent, it's your job to demonstrate positive boundaries in your own interactions with others. Showing respect for the boundaries of others — whether it's with your partner, friend, or your own parents or siblings — is an ideal way to set a valuable example for your child (Abraham, 2023).

Creating a Consistent Routine

Establishing a consistent and well-structured routine is also something you'll likely find quite helpful if you're raising a child with ODD. Routines are healthy, and for kids with ODD, they can make a huge difference. Coming up with a routine for your child (preferably *with* your child) is the best way to provide them with a sense of security. It can also be a good way to grant them some control over their surroundings (Amezcua-Patino, 2023).

When coming up with a structured schedule, consider what your child does in their average day at home — from waking up, to eating breakfast, to doing homework, to watching TV, playing games on the computer or engaging with social media. Take care to make time for sleep, meals, completing homework and chores, and leisure. Kids need this type of balance in their lives (as do we adults). Using this structured approach can help when it comes to addressing disruptive behaviors linked to ODD (Amezcua-Patino, 2023).

From a developmental standpoint, a structured routine can really help to improve your child's time-management skills. It may also instill in them a sense of responsibility, which is a big deal for kids with ODD

(Amezcua-Patino, 2023). Working with your child to come up with a routine that works for them can teach them about the importance of following set schedules when it comes to completing important tasks, like homework (i.e., it'll set them up for success in their future). This, in turn, will contribute to their growth and development, as well as teach them how to practice self-discipline.

Natural Consequences vs. Punishments

Most of the time, we have a natural inclination to protect our children. Sometimes, though, if we notice our child making a bad decision (that won't ultimately harm them *too* much), we might find ourselves thinking, *Let's see how this plays out.* The best way for many children to learn not to do something, after all, is by experiencing the consequences first-hand. If you say, "Honey, please don't stick peas in your sister's ears," your child might ask, "Why not?" and continue with this behavior.

And even if you say, "Please don't stick peas in your sister's ears because it's painful for her," a child with ODD might not have compassion (as most neurotypical children would), and might not stop. In fact, if they're aware that sticking peas in their sister's ears is causing her pain, they might feel inclined to continue doing it. That's just the nature of ODD. On the other hand, if you say something like, "Hey, don't stick peas in your sister's ears… unless you want her to cry all night long," they might actually rethink their behavior because they know that listening to their baby sister cry for hours on end is unpleasant, so they might choose to avoid engaging in behaviors that upset her. Maybe.

You might also say something like, "If you keep sticking peas in your sister's ears, you won't be allowed to play video games for a week." For a child with ODD to behave the way you want them to, they need to associate unpleasant natural consequences or punishments with their

74

bad behavior. These consequences or punishments have to create an inconvenience for them rather than someone else, like their sister. Okay, we're finished with the peas in ears example now!

How to Use Consequences and Punishments to Teach

People often use the terms "consequence" and "punishment" interchangeably when discussing discipline, but it's important to be able to distinguish between them. Punishment involves causing emotional distress — it's a way to force a child to behave as desired. Consequences, on the other hand, concern the results of a child's behavior, whether they are positive, negative, or neutral. Encouraging natural consequences is preferred, as it will help your child understand the cause-and-effect connection between their actions and the outcomes that come with them (Lund, 2019).

When addressing your child's bad behavior, try to focus on teaching rather than coercion (Lund, 2019). Remember to provide them with a clear description of what inappropriate behavior is, and try to guide them toward more positive alternatives. For example, if your child is whining about not getting ice cream, you might say, "Right now, you are talking in a whiny voice and repeatedly asking for ice cream. I need you to say 'Okay' calmly and not ask again."

If, after you address your child's whining, they throw a cup against the wall, you might say something like, "I understand that you're upset, but it's not okay to throw a cup. Since you did that, you will not have ice cream for the rest of the day. If you can find a way to calm down appropriately, you'll earn a different treat later." As you can see, teaching children through consequences establishes a cause-and-effect understanding and empowers them to take accountability for their actions (Lund, 2019).

Unlike punishment, which is exclusively applied to negative behaviors, consequences can be positive or negative (or neutral, as stated above).

Prioritizing positive consequences more frequently than negative ones can make the teaching through consequences methods we learned above more effective. This balanced approach to positive and negative consequences can not only repair your strained parent-child relationship, but might also help nurture a happier, healthier family dynamic.

Reward Systems that Actually Work

When creating a reward system for your child with ODD, remember to take their age into account. This will help you align your expectations with whatever developmental stage they're in. Dr. Kate Eshleman, a pediatric psychologist, talks about the importance of rewards when it comes to inspiring children to engage in behaviors that might not naturally appeal to them (Gordon, 2022). External rewards can act as incentives, and may even give certain tasks more meaning, which can improve your child's sense of commitment.

The chosen reward needs to be attractive, consistent, and achievable. This is why Dr. Eshleman stresses the importance of involving your child in developing the reward system. Immediate, specific feedback connected to small steps toward bigger goals is also important (this is positive reinforcement in action). For example, if your child wants a specific toy, like a Lego set, as a reward for staying in bed at bedtime or completing their homework, you can use tangible symbols (like stickers or tokens) to track their progress and let them know when they're getting close to reaching their goal. These smaller rewards will accumulate, and, eventually, your child will be allowed to get that Lego set they've been wanting. Dr. Eshleman emphasizes the need for parents to stick to the plans they've outlined in order for this system to be effective (Gordon, 2022). Remember, consistency is key!

When implementing a reward system, it's generally a good idea to focus on one or two specific behaviors first. Dr. Eshleman suggests choosing behaviors that your child understands, as well as making your expectations clear right up front. Brittany Schaffner, a crisis education supervisor, suggests identifying a specific behavior, setting realistic expectations, and being patient as your child goes through the learning process (Gordon, 2022). Involving your child in choosing the reward, providing them with clear guidance, offering specific praise, and maintaining consistency are very important aspects of this process.

Negotiating with a Strong-Willed Child

Riding the rollercoaster of parenting, especially with a strong-willed child (e.g., a child with ODD), goes beyond just learning how to say "no." Learning how to negotiate with your strong-willed child takes time and effort. You'll need to use thoughtful negotiation strategies and teach them how to be more understanding and resilient as a whole. This is no easy task, but it might help to let them engage in the occasional indulgence. That's what negotiation is all about, after all. Your child needs to be able to understand that ice cream for breakfast might be okay on their birthday, but it's not something they should expect on a regular basis.

Years ago, I took an executive negotiation class that helped to transform my outlook on saying "no." Forget the stern refusals; the game plan should involve framing denials in a positive, encouraging light. This is a paradox that echoes executive negotiation tactics, but it can be surprisingly effective in shaping your child's inner dialogues as they grow (Moore, 2021). Instead of falling headfirst into arguments with your child, try to offer them preemptive alternatives. Doing so will give them a sense of control, which is often what children with ODD lack.

Recognizing the power of control, especially when met with resistance, involves providing your child with fair warnings and giving them a say — even if it's just about choosing a number between one and ten

(Moore, 2021). Suddenly, the dreaded "no" transforms into a collaborative decision, therefore reducing your child's impulse to resist. When immediate accommodation isn't in the cards, you can agree on a future date (e.g., a birthday or Christmas) to give your child what they want. Just remember to follow through, though, as this will help build trust. Disagreements are just a part of life, and every parent has disagreements with their children at some point. As with most things, successfully negotiating with a strong-willed child is all about balance. Find the balance between saying "yes" or "no," creating a collaborative environment, and acknowledging the occasional indulgence of ice cream for breakfast, and you'll be on the right path.

Segue

Setting boundaries with a child who has ODD is probably going to be a frustrating process for you as a parent, but it's important that you stick to the boundaries you set — otherwise, your child might not take them, or you, seriously. Try to get them to understand how natural consequences and punishments correlate with their inappropriate behaviors, and don't let them walk all over you. Sophie can attest to the fact that this is easier said than done, of course, especially if you're parenting a tween or teen — but being firm and standing up to your kid with ODD when necessary will benefit both of you in the end. And by the way, it'll also benefit your mental health — which is always a plus. In the next chapter, we'll go over how to cope with your child's challenging behaviors. Parents will often "freeze" when their children act up, which is totally understandable, but with the following strategies on hand, you'll no longer have to worry about not knowing what to do in the moment.

CHAPTER 6
Coping with Challenging Behaviors

"Children need love, especially when they do not deserve it." - *Harold Hulburt,* psychiatrist at child guidance clinics

I recently met a woman who's been having some parenting challenges. Her son, Alex, is a ball of energy with a kind heart — but he's also struggling with ODD. She told me it's been a bit of a rollercoaster for her, especially when it comes to handling Alex's meltdowns. One day we were all at the park near her house. Alex, fueled by frustration, was tearing around the playground and threatening to hit other children. His fists were clenched, and you could see the intensity in his eyes. His mother tried not to panic and knew this problem would require a gentle touch.

Her first move was to create a safety net by guiding Alex away from the busy play area to a quieter spot for him to release his big feelings. Crouching down to his eye level, she tried to be a calm presence in the midst of his emotional storm. I listened in as she assured him that it was okay to feel angry, but that they needed to find a way to weather this storm together without resorting to violence. She had her toolkit ready. It was amazing to watch. Spotting a colorful butterfly nearby, she quickly redirected Alex's attention, asking if he could see it. It worked, if only for a moment. His focus shifted, and he calmed down temporarily.

This is an example of how you can cope with your child's challenging behaviors that are related to ODD. It won't help to become angry at them, nor will it help to ignore their behavior. If you can gently redirect their attention elsewhere when they're expressing their big feelings — remember, it's okay for them to express these feelings in a *controlled* environment where no one else will be hurt — then you may be able to calm them in the moment. You may be thinking, *But if I pointed out a butterfly to my kid, they probably wouldn't care.* While this may be true, it's not about the butterfly but the redirection tactic, and you never know until you try. If this redirection doesn't work, try a different redirection technique.

Once your child has achieved a calm state of mind (this might take a while), they should be able to work through their complicated emotions in a healthier way. Be sure to let them know that you're there for them no matter what, and that they don't have to deal with the storm swirling inside them alone. In this chapter, we'll talk all about effective techniques for handling tantrums, meltdowns, defiance, and aggressive behavior. Strap yourselves in and let's go!

Defusing Tantrums and Meltdowns

You've probably witnessed a kid screaming and crying in public before. Chances are, you've even had to deal with your *own* child screaming and crying in public. We can all agree that tantrums and meltdowns are no fun for anyone involved. Many assume that tantrums and meltdowns are the same thing, too, but they're actually quite different. This is why it's important for you to recognize when your child is having a tantrum and when they're having a meltdown. Often, what might look like a tantrum could actually be a meltdown, and dealing with each requires specific approaches (Morin, 2023). Let's take a closer look at these approaches below:

Tips For Defusing Tantrums

- Create a frustration signal: Talk to your kid about what it looks like when they're becoming frustrated. Come up with a signal, like pulling on your earlobe, to use when they're upset. Discuss what you both will do to calm down when you use the signal.
- Designate a calm space: Pick a spot at home as a calm space. It doesn't have to be fancy — even a favorite chair would work. Explain that it's for calming down, not as a punishment. When you use the frustration signal, your child can go there to chill out.
- Think about what's causing the tantrum: If a signal or calm space doesn't work, try to figure out why the tantrum is happening. Knowing the reason will make it easier to handle in the moment as well as help you avoid it from happening again (Morin, 2023).
- Set clear expectations: Be clear about how you want your child to behave. Use sentences like, "When you're able to be calm, we can talk." This gives your child a choice (keep in mind they won't always make the right choice!).
- Acknowledge their feelings: Even if your kid is acting out, their feelings are real. Be understanding and help them put names to their feelings.
- Praise good behavior: When your child gains control of their behavior and becomes calm, praise them. Be specific about what they did well.

Tips for Defusing Meltdowns

Meltdowns are more extreme reactions to being overwhelmed. They're different from tantrums because kids aren't in control of them (Morin, 2023). Managing meltdowns is trickier, but understanding your child's triggers can help. If you can't stop a meltdown, there are ways to respond and help your child regain control.

Before the Meltdown

- Know your child's triggers: Every child is different, so understand what sets off yours. It might be emotional overload, unexpected changes, or something else (Morin, 2023).

- Notice when it's getting worse: If you catch the signs early, you might be able to help your child calm down before a meltdown happens.

- Try to distract from the trigger: Interrupt the escalation phase with a different task or activity.

- Be patient: Talking fast and loudly can make it worse. Give your child space and time to process what you're saying.

During the Meltdown

- Assess safety: Make sure no one is hurt or in danger of being hurt.

- Be reassuring: Keep your voice and body calm, noting whether your child needs distance or a hug.

- Give some space: If possible, move to a quieter place or if you're in public, find a space.

- Tone it down: Keep things quiet and less crowded. Stand to the side if your child can't or won't move.

- Plan for afterward: Think about how to reengage with your child when the meltdown is over without triggering it again.

After the Meltdown

- Let your child recover: Give them time to collect themselves.

- Find the right time to talk: When both of you are calm, discuss what happened. Give them a heads-up before talking and keep it brief.

Managing Defiance and Opposition

We've already talked about this at length, so I'm just going to give you a brief refresher! Helping your child with ODD means using specific strategies to create a positive and organized environment. When dealing with their challenging behavior, it's important to stay calm and avoid engaging into long, drawn-out arguments. Instead, clearly communicate your expectations and do not drag out discussions.

Consistency when applying house rules will help a lot. If you accidentally break a rule, you should take responsibility for it by apologizing or taking a short break. This will set a valuable example for your child and show them that everyone in the family has to follow the same standards.

Creating a structured environment is another strategy that you might find helpful. Prioritizing things like getting enough sleep, regular exercise, and nutritious meals could positively influence your child's emotion regulation skills (# *Tips for Managing Oppositional Defiant Disorder (ODD)*, n.d.-b). As we've learned, this kind of healthy lifestyle doesn't just benefit the child with ODD; it benefits the whole family.

Segue

You know by now that coping with the challenging behaviors of a child who has ODD is easier said than done. Now that you know how to defuse tantrums and meltdowns, though, you should be well on your way to being able to teach them self-regulation skills. In fact, we'll be talking a bit about self-regulation skills in the next chapter, so stay tuned.

CHAPTER 7
Self-Regulation Skills

"To handle yourself, use your head; to handle others, use your heart." - Eleanor Roosevelt

Teaching your child how to control their thoughts and actions is critical, especially when they're struggling with something like ODD. Self-regulation is mainly about being able to control how you feel and behave during stressful situations. This isn't easy for people with ODD, but it *is* possible for them to learn self-regulation skills. Teaching these skills to a kid with ODD can make a significant difference in how they connect with others.

People who are good at self-regulation usually show specific traits — like having self-awareness, sticking to their goals no matter what, being able to adapt to different situations, and looking on the bright side of things. Being self-aware means recognizing your thoughts and feelings, which, in turn, helps you remain calm and think clearly. Being adaptable means you can handle different situations and see things from alternate points of view. As we know, kids with ODD are not often very adaptable — not naturally, anyway. But this is okay, because adaptability is a learned skill. In this chapter, I'll cover some of the best self-regulation and impulse-control skills that I've come across in my extensive research.

Self-Control and Impulse Management

Many kids, especially younger ones, often struggle with regulating impulsive behavior. It's totally normal for these children, but learning how to manage it is quite useful at any age. In fact, a lack of impulse control is often at the heart of several behavior issues (Morin, 2021). If not dealt with properly, impulsive actions can become habits and become even worse over time. For example, a 5-year-old might hit someone or throw a tantrum without thinking, while a 14-year-old might do risky stuff like sharing inappropriate pictures online or experimenting with alcohol without considering the consequences.

The good news is that you can make a big difference in helping your child improve at controlling their impulses as they grow up — even if they have ODD. Studies show that interventions focused on improving impulse control and executive function can really work. Poor impulse control is tied to making questionable decisions and having a higher risk of mental health issues (Morin, 2021). So becoming better at impulse control isn't just about avoiding harm to others or yourself – it also helps improve your child's mental health.

Communication is a large part of impulse control. Kids who find it hard to express their feelings are more likely to act impulsively (Morin, 2021). Teaching your child to recognize and talk about their emotions will help them avoid behaving impulsively as a way of expressing their feelings. Start by introducing emotion labels, like angry, sad, excited, surprised, worried, or scared. Be sure to make it clear to them that feeling angry is okay, but hitting, kicking, or yelling is not.

You'll also benefit from teaching your child problem-solving skills, as we covered earlier, because they can really help with impulse control. Encourage your child to think about different ways to solve a problem before immediately diving into it. Whether it's fixing a bike chain or figuring out a complicated math problem, getting into the habit of brainstorming and weighing different solutions helps them make more thoughtful decisions (Morin, 2021).

As for managing anger, this is something that will keep impulsive outbursts in check. Teach your child specific tricks, like taking deep breaths or doing some physical activity to release their pent-up energy (Morin, 2021). Setting clear household rules and explaining why they exist creates a structured environment that supports impulse control, too. Before entering new situations, remind your child about what's expected of them, and talk about the possible consequences if rules are broken. This way, they can make smarter choices about their behavior, and will (likely) have better impulse control over time.

How to Be a Positive Role Model or Mentor

At some point in your life, you've probably benefited from having a positive role model or mentor. Perhaps a professor became a mentor to you while you were in college, or maybe you looked to your parents as positive role models. Your child with ODD can benefit from having a positive role model or mentor, as well, and (especially while they're young), you can be that role model! Just be aware that being a role model or mentor is not easy, so I'll break down a few strategies you can use to become the role model your child needs.

Understand and Address Their Needs

Being a positive role model for a child with ODD means getting to know and addressing their specific needs. The first step is to actively listen. Many kids with ODD often feel like nobody truly understands them. By taking the time to figure out what sets off their defiant behavior, you can build a positive connection with them by showing empathy and guiding them in a different direction (Healy, n.d.). This emotional connection is critical for making progress with ODD because it tends to lessen your child's urge to defy you (and others) when they know that they are genuinely understood.

Use Teamwork to Your Advantage

When it comes to parenting (and teaching, for that matter), teamwork is a key component, especially if you're parenting or teaching a child who has ODD. The old ways of being strict and authoritative don't work as well these days. Nowadays, it's important to collaborate with others (e.g., your partner if you're a parent or your teacher's assistant if you're a teacher) and solve problems together. While some things — like hygiene and homework — are non-negotiable, there's room for flexibility in how these tasks are completed (Healy, n.d.). Giving choices and involving your child in these types of decisions can help create a sense of partnership in your relationship with them.

Celebrate the Small Things

We talked about this earlier, but I'm happy to reiterate, once again, the importance of celebrating even the smallest steps that your child makes toward being cooperative and productive. Celebrating even small victories will help encourage positive changes in your child's behavior. Acknowledging and praising little improvements, like when they do their chores without resisting, for example, can help to create a positive association with these types of actions in their mind. This positive reinforcement is the key to building a more cooperative and productive relationship with your child overall (Healy, n.d.).

Teach Your Kid about Problem-Solving

Problem-solving is a big part of managing ODD. Children with ODD often default to saying "no" and resisting tasks. Empowering them by involving them in figuring out solutions, like making homework more enjoyable, for example, can help a great deal. Try to keep this motto, derived from a quote by Socrates, in mind: "The kids who are hardest to love often need it the most." If you're able to embrace this idea, you might just have an easier time creating a caring and understanding environment for your child who has ODD. Figuring out what motivates them is also important. The more motivated your child is to solve a problem, the more likely they are to be able to solve it on their own (Healy, n.d.).

The Role of Hobbies and Interests

Hobbies and other interests are quite beneficial for a child's growth. There are significant advantages to encouraging your child with ODD to find hobbies or join clubs (*How Hobbies Benefit Children and Their Learning Experience.*, n.d.). First, hobbies can provide kids with stress relief (just like they do for us adults). Doing things they enjoy allows their minds and bodies to relax.

Hobbies also make kids better at thinking. Even though children often can't focus for a long time (especially true for kids with ODD or ADHD), doing fun activities helps them concentrate more. It builds up their focus, reasoning, problem-solving, and thinking skills. Hobbies also teach them about discipline, patience, and the time it takes to learn and become skilled at something. For example, if your child loves building things with blocks, they'll spend time figuring it out. As their parent, you can guide them, and this will help them learn important life skills (*How Hobbies Benefit Children and Their Learning Experience.*, n.d.).

If your child spends a lot of time engaging in their hobbies, it can be a valuable exercise in creativity for them, as well. There are plenty of hobbies that allow kids to be creative, express themselves, and see things in different ways. Who knows, maybe your kid will become a future inventor or a great writer one day! Getting involved in hobbies that require teamwork, like playing sports or going camping, can help kids make friends and feel good about themselves. Working together and talking with their friends to reach their goals teaches them about caring for others and being part of a team (*How Hobbies Benefit Children and Their Learning Experience.*, n.d.). Doing outdoor hobbies also helps keep kids healthy and happy, since they get plenty of exercise.

Hobbies aren't just for fun, though — they teach kids more about life outside of school. Engaging in hobbies is a great way for them to discover new talents. With your help, they might even be able to become really good at something they love. Hobbies also prevent kids from feeling bored and becoming cranky. They are excellent distractions, and usually help keep kids from becoming restless. Not only that, but hobbies can help kids learn how to manage their time more effectively because they learn how to balance their time between playing, working (i.e., doing school assignments), and resting. (*How Hobbies Benefit Children and Their Learning Experience.*, n.d.).

Segue

As with most of the techniques discussed throughout this book, it will take time for your child to learn how to self-regulate. This process probably won't be easy for them, which is why it's important for you to talk with them about why it'll be worth it. The more you talk about this with them, the more they'll understand why they need to be able to self-regulate. In the next chapter, we'll wrap up and talk more about celebrating progress. This is just as important as anything else, so keep reading to discover some ways you can celebrate your child's progress.

CHAPTER 8
Celebrating Progress

"A child must know that he is a miracle, that since the beginning of the world there hasn't been, and until the end of the world there will not be, another child like him." - *Pablo Casals*, world-renowned cellist and composer

W hen we talk about recognizing achievements, we often connect it with the business world. But celebrating milestones isn't just for professionals — parents and teachers can use awards to appreciate the accomplishments of all kids, including those who are dealing with ODD. This kind of recognition goes beyond the usual standards, and it allows parents and teachers to cheer for the hard work and dedication that a child with ODD is putting into their success (*Recognizing Every Day Milestones with Kids | Awards4U*, n.d.).

When parenting a child with ODD, acknowledging milestones becomes especially meaningful. Awards, like medals, can be used to call attention to not just the usual successes but also the less-conventional ones. This will help to emphasize the importance of effort and determination (instead of just focusing on grades, for example) (*Recognizing Every Day Milestones with Kids | Awards4U*, n.d.). This way, your child will feel valued, noticed, and motivated to continue making positive contributions.

Much like how employees desire recognition from their employers for their hard work, children also want acknowledgment for their achievements. It's not just about doing well once; it's about wanting to do well again and again in the hope of receiving continued recognition (*Recognizing Every Day Milestones with Kids | Awards4U*, n.d.). Parents and teachers should watch for specific milestones that might not be the usual celebrated ones but are still important to a child's growth.

For example, you'll definitely want to acknowledge when your child is taking responsibility at home. Even though doing chores might seem like a small thing to you, praising your child's effort in completing them helps to build their sense of responsibility, as well as their organizational skills (*Recognizing Every Day Milestones with Kids | Awards4U*, n.d.). For younger kids, simple rewards like a trip to the park or a special treat can be powerful acknowledgments, and reinforce the idea that hard work is valuable.

As most of us already know, kids grow in areas beyond the classroom. They may excel in sports, leadership, or even just being a good friend. Celebrating achievements in these areas is just as important as celebrating academic achievements (*Recognizing Every Day Milestones with Kids | Awards4U*, n.d.). In cases where giving physical awards might not be practical, more affordable alternatives — like sticker charts or point systems — could work well when it comes to recognizing accomplishments.

Another important aspect is acknowledging your child's improvement. Every child learns at their own pace, and appreciating their hard work is more valuable than just focusing on them being the smartest kid in the room (*Recognizing Every Day Milestones with Kids | Awards4U*, n.d.). Children with ODD face unique challenges, so it's important to celebrate their progress and achievements in specific subjects at school as well as overall improvements in their responsibilities at home.

These examples are just the tip of the iceberg. The possibilities for recognizing everyday or unconventional milestones for children are endless. Whether it's a simple thumbs-up, a small gesture, or a real award, genuine recognition is incredibly valuable. Offering words of encouragement will let your child know that their hard work has been noticed, and will help reinforce the idea that their efforts, both personal and academic, matter.

Parenting after ODD: A Lifelong Journey

Allow me to share a couple of stories I came across while reading about the journey of parenting a child with ODD. When Alison Thompson's son, Daniel, was almost four, she candidly wrote in her diary that she believed he was the "original child from hell" (Frye, 2023). She described days filled with turmoil, where Daniel would knock things down, throw tantrums, and be generally aggressive — sometimes hitting his family members and making holes in the walls. Similarly, Kim Abraham, in Michigan, faced an ongoing battle with her son, Nathan, who refused to go to school, stole things, and seemed hell-bent on breaking the rules (Frye, 2023).

Both Daniel and Nathan were eventually diagnosed with ODD (as you probably guessed). Along with ODD, they both had ADHD, and Daniel had Asperger's Syndrome. They both spent their childhoods being expelled from different schools, getting into trouble with the law, and fighting with their parents daily. Alison noticed Daniel's disruptive behavior from a very young age. She even described him as an "angry baby" who rarely slept. As he grew older, his mood swings and impulsivity became even more pronounced. Kim viewed Nathan as her most difficult child, since he frequently broke the rules and pushed boundaries with everyone around him. By the time Nathan reached middle school, he was constantly in trouble, and the situation escalated with time (Frye, 2023).

Nathan's diagnosis of ODD shed light on the reasons behind his behavior. Despite going to multiple therapists and Kim trying many different strategies, traditional discipline methods were simply ineffective (Frye, 2023). Nathan's defiance left Kim feeling helpless as a parent. Meanwhile, Daniel's tantrums led to another school expulsion and a subsequent diagnosis of ADHD, ODD, and Asperger's Syndrome.

For Daniel, medication, including Ritalin and Equasym, had a noticeable impact. This seemed to help him learn some strategies to control his emotions and anger. Although he still faced challenges, a pupil referral unit in the UK provided him with a supportive environment and introduced a system to prevent meltdowns by offering rewards for good behavior (Frye, 2023). Kim took a different approach with Nathan, and created a behavioral therapy system of her own design. Instead of using traditional consequences, she focused on consequences she could control, and eventually established a household-wide system of reciprocity (Frye, 2023). Nathan initially resisted but eventually began to change his behavior, having learned that relationships are a two-way street.

Despite numerous setbacks, both Daniel and Nathan have made significant progress. Daniel, now 18, works in a restaurant and has found unexpected success in helping refugees in Europe. Nathan, despite his mother's initial concerns, is now a successful roofer with a family of his own (Frye, 2023). Both mothers have written books about their experiences, which I'd highly recommend reading. Their experiences show that parenting a child with ODD is a lifelong journey — it's not something that ever "ends," but something to which you learn how to adapt (and help your child adapt to over time). While things might feel hopeless right now, don't worry. In time, you will figure out a system that works well for both you and your child, just as Alison and Kim did.

Advocating for Your Child's Needs

Finding out that your child might be dealing with ODD (or a similar learning or psychiatric issue) is never easy, but as a parent, there are plenty of things you can do to make sure they receive the right support at home *and* at school. Parents of kids with ODD often find themselves advocating for their kids a lot — mainly because kids with ODD get into trouble quite often. Being a strong advocate involves talking openly with your child. Research shows that having positive talks with your parents helps you make better choices, do well in school, and feel good about yourself (Koplewicz, 2023). So, start by asking your child direct questions about school to create a supportive atmosphere for them.

It's also important to realize that your child might behave differently at home than they do at school. Chatting with their teacher might help you gain a better understanding of how they're actually doing in the classroom. Teachers spend a lot of time with your children, so they usually have helpful insights. Parent-teacher conferences can be quite useful, and having questions ready could be a great way to address your concerns, set goals, and discuss any special-education services that might help your child (Koplewicz, 2023).

As a parent, it's your responsibility to take the lead when it comes to finding the right support for your child. Don't wait for parent-teacher conferences to deal with an issue; instead, ask for a thorough evaluation and information about special-education services as soon as you notice there's a problem (Koplewicz, 2023). Federal law says schools should provide education in the least restrictive environment possible, which is meant to make it so that kids with learning or psychiatric issues receive the help they need. The system isn't perfect, though, so be prepared to fight for your child if necessary.

If your child needs special-education services, put your request in writing. Send a letter to the school's special-education person, explaining your worries and asking for an evaluation. Meeting with the evaluators to review the results can also be helpful, since it will give you more information and you'll have the opportunity to clarify or discuss any disagreements. I'd also recommend keeping an eye on your child's moods, because it can be difficult to tell when a child is truly displaying ODD symptoms (especially when they're younger). If you're even a little concerned, don't be afraid to be pushy and persistent in order to get the help your child needs.

Inspiring Hope and Resilience

When you scroll through social media and see parents proudly sharing their kids' accomplishments, it might make you feel like you're doing something wrong. While Karen's kid is a soccer star and on the honor roll, your kid is throwing cartons of eggs around at the grocery store. It's only natural to be a little disappointed or envious and wonder if there's something you should be doing differently as a parent. My friend recently opened up to me about the struggle of witnessing friends' posts about their academically thriving kids while her own son struggled with nightly homework-related meltdowns. I reminded her that people usually only show the good parts of their lives on social media, and while these kids that her friends are posting about may be "thriving" academically, it's possible they could be struggling in other areas.

Raising a child with ODD stirs up a mix of emotions — hurt, anger, frustration, embarrassment, and fear. In the midst of these difficult moments, it's important that you're able to realize that strengths exist alongside the challenges that come with an ODD personality (Abraham, 2023). Amid the emotional struggle of dealing with your child's defiance, there are positive traits to discover, as well. Shifting your perspective, of course, will require you to be receptive and willing to learn. You might even learn something about your child with ODD that truly surprises and amazes you. Let's take a look below at the strengths of kids with ODD to give you an idea of what to look out for in your own child.

Creativity

One strength that stands out is the creativity that kids with ODD often possess. Their resourcefulness tends to shine when they chase after their goals, so you should always encourage them to do so. My friend's son, Tyler, for instance, is now a brilliant man with a knack for fixing things, but he often clashed with his parents as a tween and teen. Despite the challenges that his family went through, Tyler's creative problem-solving didn't go unnoticed. His parents eventually embraced his resourcefulness, and this led to him starting a successful business repairing and selling antiques.

Determination

Determination is another remarkable strength that you're bound to see in your child who has ODD. Unlike those who go with the flow, these kids tend to display a fierce determination to swim against the current (Abraham, 2023). When Tyler was 15, he would be in constant disagreement with his parents, and this is ultimately what drove him to focus on his passion. Despite criticism from family friends and outsiders (i.e., those who just didn't understand), Tyler's commitment to repairing things ultimately shaped him into a compassionate person who enjoyed helping others. Today, his parents are quite proud of him, but they should be proud of themselves, too. After all, they believed in him no matter what.

Taking the Road Less Traveled

Oppositional defiant kids will often become trailblazers, which means they'll usually decide to take unconventional paths that challenge societal norms (Abraham, 2023). Robert Downey Jr., Steve Jobs, and

Elon Musk all showcase the success that can come from taking "the road less traveled." Teens with ODD, in particular, will often follow this road because it's a way for them to defy established norms and go against societal expectations. This isn't always a good thing, but it *can* be. As long as you can guide your child, tween, or teen toward a "road less traveled" that isn't *dangerous*, they will likely benefit from the personal growth.

In order to recognize these strengths in your child, you must confront the prevailing fear that's often tied to raising a child with ODD. This fear may stem from concerns about societal judgments or your child's safety and well-being, both of which are completely understandable. But it's critical to accept your child for who they are. Any attempts to alter their personality will only perpetuate the daily challenges that you and they have been going through. In therapy sessions, kids with ODD will often express a desire for acceptance, which simply goes to show how difficult it can be for parents to embrace their kids without trying to fundamentally change who they are. Acceptance is a daily challenge, unfortunately, so in order to truly accept your child, you'll have to let go of the impulse to control and instead embrace their unique identity (Abraham, 2023).

Beyond ODD: A Bright Future for Your Child

As we have learned, helping your child navigate ODD is going to involve taking proactive steps and asking for help from healthcare professionals. Finding treatment as early as possible is extremely important, since it can help prevent ODD symptoms from worsening as your child grows. Be sure to attend all scheduled appointments with your child's healthcare provider. Family therapy might also be suggested for additional support, but this won't always be the case. Work closely with your child's healthcare provider to build a care team that's specifically tailored to your child's needs. This team might include a counselor at their school, a regular therapist, a social worker, a psychologist, and a psychiatrist.

Effective communication is also key when it comes to managing ODD. Share information about your child's conduct disorder with others, and collaborate with the healthcare provider — as well as your child's school — to come up with a treatment plan that works. If ODD significantly affects your child's performance at school, you might explore available protections and accommodations under the Americans with Disabilities Act (ADA) or Section 504 of the Civil Rights Act (Admin, 2021). Consult with your child's teacher and school principal to gather more information and take the necessary steps. If you're feeling overwhelmed or stressed, discussing these emotions with your child's healthcare provider might help, because they can provide you with recommendations for caregiver support groups and other resources.

Recognizing when to reach out to the healthcare provider is vital. If your child is experiencing symptoms like extreme depression, fear, anxiety, or anger toward themselves or others, feels out of control, hears or sees things others don't, or displays behavior that raises concerns from friends, family, or teachers, reach out to their healthcare provider immediately (Admin, 2021). If necessary, call 911 in the event of an emergency. Most of us know this, of course, but it can be easy to forget in a turbulent moment, so it's worth mentioning!

In order to ensure your child has a bright future, keep in mind how ODD works. As I've stated plenty of times now, ODD is a behavior disorder that's characterized by defiance, hostility, and uncooperativeness in children. It may stem from developmental problems or learned behaviors. Diagnosis is typically made by a mental health expert, and therapy aimed at improving relationships with others is the primary treatment currently available. As we learned earlier, depending on accompanying issues, like ADHD, medication may also be considered (Admin, 2021).

Remember to prepare for visits with your child's healthcare provider by understanding the purpose of each visit, writing down any questions you have, and recording new diagnoses, medications, or treatment plans (Admin, 2021). Don't be afraid to ask about alternative treatment methods, either. There are a number of things that could help your child cope with their ODD symptoms, and medication and therapy isn't always the answer. Keep track of information about follow-up appointments and how to contact your child's healthcare provider after office hours if an emergency occurs.

Segue

We've just about reached the end of this book, so give yourself a hand for staying with it! The fact that you picked up this book in the first place shows that you're truly committed to helping your child break free from their ODD symptoms (or, at the very least, you'll be able to help them cope with their symptoms more effectively). More than anything, I want you to know that it's possible for a child with ODD to have a bright future. Do *not* listen to anyone who says otherwise, and just continue to believe in your child. They have the power to take back their lives from the torment of ODD, and you have the power to be the beacon that guides them through the darkness.

Conclusion

You know, better than anyone, that raising a child with ODD is never going to be a walk in the park. Here's what most people don't realize, though: That's not a bad thing. As a parent, the best thing you can do for your child is love them unconditionally and continue to be there for them through thick and thin. While it may sometimes be hard to love a child unconditionally who has ODD, you will show an incredible amount of strength by choosing to love them despite all of the stress and pain they might be inadvertently causing you. Please remember, it's not their fault.

Let's take a moment to go over everything we've learned, shall we? You have a comprehensive toolbelt now, so you should feel a bit more confident about helping your child cope with their ODD symptoms. Naturally, they are still going to have bad days. We *all* have bad days every now and then. Hug them close and let them know they're loved. Even if they try to wriggle away from you, deep down they'll appreciate your affection for them. At the beginning of this book, we discussed what ODD is and the intricacies of ODD typology. We also covered the behavioral, physical, cognitive, and psychosocial symptoms of ODD. From there, we moved on to talking about the ODD diagnostic process and the importance of finding the right healthcare professionals for your child's treatment.

Next, we discussed how holistic parenting works, as well as some strategies you can use to practice self-care. We then talked about nurturing emotional intelligence and cultivating compassion in your child. From there, we moved on to the importance of setting boundaries and creating a consistent routine for your child. We learned how to defuse tantrums and meltdowns, and how to be a positive role model. Finally, we talked about celebrating your child's small wins and advocating for them to make sure they receive the best treatment possible.

I realize this is a lot of information, and it may be somewhat overwhelming. Feel free to revisit any section of this book whenever you're feeling lost or panicked as you parent a child with ODD. Remember that you have the power and know-how to be there for them in exactly the way they need you to be. It's all about being confident and knowing how to use these tools at the drop of a hat. You've got this, and I believe in you!

Don't forget it takes time for your child to adapt to their new routine. You're unlikely to see immediate changes, but that doesn't mean that the strategies you're using aren't working. I sincerely hope you've enjoyed this book and will find it helpful. Feel free to leave a review on Amazon and share it with your friends if you think they'd find it helpful in their own parenting journey! Now go be the parent your child deserves.

Resources

5 Steps to Nurture Emotional Intelligence in Your Child. (n.d.). https://www.ahaparenting.com/read/steps-to-encourage

Admin, R. (2021, December 15). *A bright future for every child*. Restoration of the Dignity of Womanhood. https://rotdow.org/2021/12/15/a-bright-future-for-every-child/

Articles. (n.d.). https://www.cedars-sinai.org/health-library/diseases-and-conditions---pediatrics/o/oppositional-defiant-disorder-odd-in-children.html

Belmont Behavioral Health System. (2020, November 12). *Causes, Signs, & Effects of ODD*. https://www.belmontbehavioral.com/disorders/odd/causes-effects/

Boylan, K. (2014, February 1). *The many faces of oppositional defiant disorder*. PubMed Central (PMC). https://www.ncbi.nlm.nih.gov/pmc/articles/PMC3917664/

Bsn, S. a. W. R. (2022, June 2). *Understanding ADHD and ODD*. Psych Central. https://psychcentral.com/adhd/adhd-odd#diagnosis

Digital, A. (2022, May 26). *Conduct Disorder vs. ODD*. The Recovery Village Drug and Alcohol Rehab. https://www.therecoveryvillage.com/mental-health/disruptive-behavior-disorder/conduct-disorder-vs-odd/

Frye, D. (2022, April 1). Back from the brink: Two families' stories of oppositional defiant disorder. *ADDitude*. https://www.additudemag.com/oppositional-defiant-disorder-adhd-family-stories/amp/

Garey, J., PsyD, S. a. L., & Lcsw, C. W. (2023, October 12). *Teaching kids how to deal with conflict*. Child Mind Institute. https://childmind.org/article/teaching-kids-how-to-deal-with-conflict/

Garey, J., & Rouse, M. H., PhD. (2023, October 30). *Why Self-Care is essential to Parenting*. Child Mind Institute. https://childmind.org/article/fighting-caregiver-burnout-special-needs-kids/

Gonos, K. (2021, August 10). *Cultivating Empathy and Compassion | Andrew Weil, M.D.* DrWeil.com. https://www.drweil.com/blog/spontaneous-happiness/cultivating-empathy-and-compassion/

Gordon, S. (2022, November 30). *How to create an effective reward system for kids*. Verywell Family. https://www.verywellfamily.com/how-to-create-a-reward-system-for-kids-that-works-1094752

Harper, C. (2023, June 22). How to Build a Support System for Your Mental Health. *MyWellbeing*. https://mywellbeing.com/therapy-101/how-to-build-a-support-system

How hobbies benefit children and their learning experience. (n.d.). Wyeth Nutrition ParenTeam Malaysia. https://wyethnutrition.com.my/why-are-hobbies-important-for-kids

Kramer, C. (2019, June 12). *Autism and ODD: What You Need to Know*. The Autism Site News. https://blog.theautismsite.greatergood.com/oppositional-defiant-disorder/

Lcsw, A. J. M. (2019, December 3). *3 Tips for parenting as a United Front - North Shore Family Services*. North Shore Family Services. https://northshorefamilyservices.com/3-tips-for-parenting-as-a-united-front/

Lcsw, A. M. (2020, September 30). *Discipline for kids with oppositional defiant disorder*. Verywell Family.

https://www.verywellfamily.com/oppositional-defiant-disorder-discipline-1094924

Lcsw, A. M. (2021, October 25). *Impulse control techniques that work for children*. Verywell Family. https://www.verywellfamily.com/ways-to-teach-children-impulse-control-1095035

Lindhiem, O., Bennett, C. B., Hipwell, A. E., & Pardini, D. A. (2015). Beyond symptom counts for diagnosing oppositional defiant disorder and conduct disorder? *Journal of Abnormal Child Psychology*, *43*(7), 1379–1387. https://doi.org/10.1007/s10802-015-0007-x

Lmsw, K. A. (2021, May 28). *ODD Kids - Managing Verbal Abuse and Entitlement Mentality*. Empowering Parents. https://www.empoweringparents.com/article/when-odd-kids-entitlement-mentality-and-verbal-abuse-collide/

Lmsw, K. A. (2022, December 13). *The strengths of oppositional, defiant (ODD) kids*. Empowering Parents. https://www.empoweringparents.com/article/strengths-oppositional-defiant-child/

Lovering, N. (2021, September 29). *Treating Oppositional Defiant Disorder (ODD)*. Psych Central. https://psychcentral.com/disorders/oppositional-defiant-disorder-treatment

Lund, A. (2020, February 27). *The difference between consequences and punishments*. Smarter Parenting. https://www.smarterparenting.com/parenting-skills/effective-negative-consequences/the-difference-between-consequences-and-punishments/

Masters, T. (2021, July 2). *Common myths about Oppositional Defiant Disorder (ODD)*. Edge Foundation. https://edgefoundation.org/common-myths-about-oppositional-defiant-disorder-odd/

Moore, S. R. (2023, June 13). Negotiation with Kids: 5 Ways to Skip the Power Struggle - Dandelion Seeds Positive Parenting. *Dandelion Seeds Positive Parenting*. https://dandelion-seeds.com/positive-parenting/negotiation-with-kids/

Morin, A. (2023, October 5). *Taming tantrums vs. managing meltdowns*. Understood. https://www.understood.org/en/articles/taming-tantrums-vs-managing-meltdowns

National University. (2022, August 17). What is Social Emotional Learning (SEL): Why It Matters. *National University*. https://www.nu.edu/blog/social-emotional-learning-sel-why-it-matters-for-educators/amp/

Navigating insurance | Immune Deficiency Foundation. (n.d.). https://primaryimmune.org/living-primary-immunodeficiency/navigating-insurance

Notification. (n.d.). https://www.tlc.com/parenting/siblings-help-develop-empathy-in-each-other--study-says

Oppositional defiant disorder (ODD) - Diagnosis and treatment - Mayo Clinic. (2023a, January 4). https://www.mayoclinic.org/diseases-conditions/oppositional-defiant-disorder/diagnosis-treatment/drc-20375837

Oppositional defiant disorder (ODD) - Diagnosis and treatment - Mayo Clinic. (2023b, January 4). https://www.mayoclinic.org/diseases-conditions/oppositional-defiant-disorder/diagnosis-treatment/drc-20375837#:~:text=Medicines%20alone%20generally%20aren't,Parenting%20skills%20training

Oppositional defiant Disorder (ODD) in children. (2023, May 31). Johns Hopkins Medicine. https://www.hopkinsmedicine.org/health/conditions-and-diseases/oppositional-defiant-disorder

Oppositional defiant Disorder treatment. (2023, February 16). New Haven Treatment Center. https://newhavenrtc.com/odd-treatment/oppositional-defiant-disorder-treatment/

Pardee, L. (2023, August 17). What's Your Parenting Style? *Parents.* https://www.parents.com/parenting/better-parenting/style/parenting-styles-explained/

Professional, C. C. M. (n.d.). *Oppositional Defiant Disorder (ODD).* Cleveland Clinic. https://my.clevelandclinic.org/health/diseases/9905-oppositional-defiant-disorder

Recognizing Every Day Milestones with Kids | Awards4U. (n.d.). https://awards4u.com/blog/recognizing-every-day-milestones-kids

Resilience: Build skills to endure hardship. (2022, July 14). Mayo Clinic. https://www.mayoclinic.org/tests-procedures/resilience-training/in-depth/resilience/art-20046311

Rose, R. (2023, June 23). *Sibling empathy and compassion - your perfect dreams.* Your Perfect Dreams. https://www.yourperfectdreams.com/sibling-empathy-and-compassion/

Taking Care of YOU: Self-Care for Family Caregivers - Family Caregiver Alliance. (2023, January 11). Family Caregiver Alliance. https://www.caregiver.org/resource/taking-care-you-self-care-family-caregivers/

Tee-Melegrito, R. A. (2023, January 9). *Treatment for oppositional defiant disorder.* https://www.medicalnewstoday.com/articles/treatment-for-oppositional-defiance-disorder

What is early intervention? (2020, May 13). Early Intervention Foundation. https://www.eif.org.uk/why-it-matters/what-is-early-intervention